Cambridge Elements

Elements in the Gothic
edited by
Dale Townshend
Manchester Metropolitan University
Angela Wright
University of Sheffield

COASTAL GOTHIC, 1719–2020

Jimmy Packham
University of Birmingham

Shaftesbury Road, Cambridge CB2 8EA, United Kingdom

One Liberty Plaza, 20th Floor, New York, NY 10006, USA

477 Williamstown Road, Port Melbourne, VIC 3207, Australia

314–321, 3rd Floor, Plot 3, Splendor Forum, Jasola District Centre, New Delhi – 110025, India

103 Penang Road, #05–06/07, Visioncrest Commercial, Singapore 238467

Cambridge University Press is part of Cambridge University Press & Assessment, a department of the University of Cambridge.

We share the University's mission to contribute to society through the pursuit of education, learning and research at the highest international levels of excellence.

www.cambridge.org
Information on this title: www.cambridge.org/9781009548205

DOI: 10.1017/9781009433730

© Jimmy Packham 2025

This publication is in copyright. Subject to statutory exception and to the provisions of relevant collective licensing agreements, no reproduction of any part may take place without the written permission of Cambridge University Press & Assessment.

When citing this work, please include a reference to the DOI 10.1017/9781009433730

First published 2025

A catalogue record for this publication is available from the British Library

ISBN 978-1-009-54820-5 Hardback
ISBN 978-1-009-43375-4 Paperback
ISSN 2634-8721 (online)
ISSN 2634-8713 (print)

Cambridge University Press & Assessment has no responsibility for the persistence or accuracy of URLs for external or third-party internet websites referred to in this publication and does not guarantee that any content on such websites is, or will remain, accurate or appropriate.

For EU product safety concerns, contact us at Calle de José Abascal, 56, 1°, 28003 Madrid, Spain, or email eugpsr@cambridge.org

Coastal Gothic, 1719–2020

Elements in the Gothic

DOI: 10.1017/9781009433730
First published online: December 2025

Jimmy Packham
University of Birmingham
Author for correspondence: Jimmy Packham, j.packham@bham.ac.uk

Abstract: Littoral zones such as haunted shorelines, oppressively expansive beaches, and the crumbling edgelands around coastal cliffs have been an indelible feature of the Gothic literary tradition since the eighteenth century. They are frequently portrayed as strange, interstitial realms, sites of epistemic and existential precarity, of wreckage and uncanny returns, poised between the homely and unhomely, whose intense openness to the world(s) beyond contends uneasily (yet valuably) with the imagined integrity of selves and nations: it is a region, above all, of unsettlement. Coastal Gothic, 1719–2020 offers the first long-form examination of the coastal Gothic. Focusing on British and Irish Gothic authors and on the fraught political and human histories of the coastline, this Element examines the function of littoral terror, hauntings, and uncanny encounters as a means of unsettling pervasive conceptions of identity at national, regional, and individual levels.

This Element also has a video abstract:
www.cambridge.org/GOTH_Packham_abstract

Keywords: the Gothic, coasts, seaside, haunted shores, the uncanny

© Jimmy Packham 2025

ISBNs: 9781009548205 (HB), 9781009433754 (PB), 9781009433730 (OC)
ISSNs: 2634-8721 (online), 2634-8713 (print)

Contents

1 Introduction: Haunted Shores   1

2 Archipelagic Gothic and the Seaside   16

3 War and the Coastal Gothic   31

4 Migration and the Coastal Uncanny   47

5 Conclusion: Lighthouses, Wreckage, and the Gothic   63

   References   70

1 Introduction: Haunted Shores

Walking one day along a beach, of which he firmly believes he has sole possession, Robinson Crusoe finds himself 'Thunder-struck', once more all at sea in the world; it is, he says, 'as if I had seen an Apparition', and he quickly becomes 'terrify'd to the last Degree' (Defoe 1994: 112). Famously, the source of this excessive and debilitating feeling – of this distinctly Gothic affect that Sarah Tindal Kareem refers to as Crusoe's 'sublime terror' (Kareem 2014: 98) – is a single footprint that Crusoe has stumbled upon, impressed in the soft littoral sand of the shoreline at the margins of the island on which he has been shipwrecked, and which he has subsequently claimed for himself (Figure 1). This moment, I argue, is emblematic of and indeed inaugurates a mode of writing this Element will define as the 'coastal Gothic', a term which not only refers to the many coastal episodes to be found within the Gothic tradition, but which also indicates a way of perceiving the coast and one's relationship to it, which can be explicated via the critical methodologies and vocabularies associated with Gothic studies.

Crusoe's mind runs amok in its quest to explain the footprint and what it portends. 'Sometimes I fancy'd it must be the Devil' (Defoe 1994: 112), he says, before reasoning that it is probably 'some more dangerous Creature' (113) – namely, cannibals from neighbouring lands. Crusoe speculates, too, that these fears are 'a meer Chimera of my own' (115) and that the footprint might in fact be his, and that he has in effect haunted himself. The discovery at the beach turns Crusoe's world upside down. 'Serving as a warning of alien power', writes Srinivas Aravamudan, 'the sighting reintroduces human agency. Where the sand ought to have been as smooth as a tabula rasa, Crusoe finds the superimposition of culture' (Aravamudan 1999: 71). For two years, Crusoe is haunted by the uncertainty that inheres within this footprint, this ambiguous signifier of a culture that may or may not be his own. Crusoe pictures himself as somehow embattled against forces he cannot quite imagine or locate, and begins, from this moment, to speak of his home as his 'Castle' ('for so I think I call'd it ever after this' (Defoe 1994: 112)).

The shore provides a vulnerable point of entry or incursion into Crusoe's world. Yet Crusoe should know this. After all, he was washed ashore several years prior to the appearance of the footprint and has since colonised the island: it is not beyond the bounds of possibility that someone else might find themselves wrecked and stranded here. In fact, one of the things this might prompt us to think about is what duties Crusoe, a castaway himself, might owe someone who has washed ashore on a part of the globe to which he has laid claim. In any case, the little nation of which Crusoe imagines himself the sole citizen and

"I STOOD LIKE ONE THUNDERSTRUCK."

Figure 1 'I stood like one thunderstruck'. Illustration by Walter Paget (Defoe 1896: facing 110). Courtesy of The University of Florida George A. Smathers Libraries.

overlord is seemingly threatened from without, and it is the intangibility of this threat that most unsettles Defoe's protagonist. The shore is the ideal space in which to dramatise this existential crisis, which is also a crisis of belonging and community, of the home and the unhomely. The presence of an Other is apprehended because of the imprint of a foot on the sand: the beach retains a strange, ghostly after-image of this figure. If Crusoe begins to speak of his 'Castle' in order to psychologically reassert the security of his home and the control and authority he exerts there, the shoreline nevertheless reminds him that this idea of control, this feeling of security, is fragile, perhaps even illusory.

1.1 Crusoe's Footprint

I begin with these reflections on the most famous moment from Daniel Defoe's *Robinson Crusoe* (1719) in order to set up several of the claims foundational to this Element, which examines the role of the coast in the Gothic literary tradition from the eighteenth to the twenty-first century, with a particular focus on British and Irish Gothic authors. At the heart of *Coastal Gothic* is the assertion that littoral settings – beaches, coasts, shores, tidal estuaries and causeways, ports and harbours – are central and essential to the Gothic: these fine and fragile margins of land where terrestrial stability gives way to oceanic fluidity have shaped the Gothic since the genre's development in the eighteenth century. Littoral geographies are as intrinsic to the Gothic as are the dilapidated abbey, the crumbling castle, subterranean labyrinths, and sublime mountain vistas, all of which are to date more firmly embedded than coastal settings in the critical vocabularies associated with Gothic literary studies. As I elaborate over the course of this Element, the terror generated by the coast is frequently quite distinct from the terrors located in or enabled by more familiar Gothic settings. For instance, the beach's 'sublime terror', to recall Kareem's words, is not rooted in the Burkean obscurity of darkness or a suggestive Walpolean gloomth. Nor does it routinely operate via 'a fearful sense of inheritance in time with a claustrophobic sense of enclosure in space', to pick up Chris Baldick's influential account of 'the Gothic effect' (Baldick 1992: xix). Instead, Gothic terror is founded in an obscurity emanating from an unsettling and sun-drenched visibility. There are few shadows and dark corners whereby terror might conceal itself at the beach: it must come into the open.

In *Coastal Gothic*, I argue that the coast offers writers of the Gothic a productive space in which to examine and consolidate forms of national identity and individual subjectivity. This Element is therefore especially attuned to the frequently fraught human and political histories of coastal regions and the archipelagic interconnectedness of England, Ireland, Scotland, and Wales, tying

Gothic coastal literature into historic and prevailing political discourses associated with the terrors of a penetrable coastline, horrifyingly and yet necessarily open to the world(s) beyond. *Coastal Gothic* examines how the Gothic dramatises competing claims made on coastal regions, claims which generate forms of littoral ambivalence by which the coast's literal, ecological precarity is evocatively echoed in various unsettled ideological and political conceptions of this region. Reading the 'Gothic coast', then, does not merely help us better understand Britain's and Ireland's Gothic traditions by placing great emphasis on a central but relatively under-examined setting. More than this, reading for 'Gothic coasts' shows how careful scrutiny of this tradition enables us to better appreciate the Gothic histories that exist, in very real ways, at the limits of the nation. That is, we see how the coast is narrated in cultural and political discourse as a fundamentally 'Gothic' zone – a space that teeters on the brink between self and Other, the familiar and the foreign, homely 'here' and *unheimlich* elsewhere, a site of pleasurable recreation but shadowed at all times by the possibility of wreckage, unexpected washings ashore, and haunting returns.

For reasons I am beginning to elaborate here, we can see *Robinson Crusoe* as a text that stands at the head of a coastal Gothic tradition. As Defoe makes abundantly clear throughout his novel, the coast is a persistent site of existential danger and haunting terror, especially for an errant colonial voyager like Crusoe. The footprint gestures towards a history that is, as Aravamudan argues, 'irretrievable': it '*initiates* the open question of its own history and interpretation' and 'deictically hints at past and future while generating a trauma that deterritorializes the novel's protagonist, threatening his property, propriety, and very sense of self' (Aravamudan 1999: 71–72). This footprint is a Gothic cipher, whose cryptic ambiguities are enhanced by Crusoe's – and possibly Defoe's and the reader's – understanding of the beach as *tabula rasa*. The supposed blankness of the beach exists in part because of the action of the tides, performing a twice-daily erasure of the tracks left on coastal sands: as another sign of the coast's receptivity to the Gothic mode, the coast is a potent site of narrative instability and unsettlement. This blankness also extends, however, from the fact that the beach is largely a culturally constructed environment evacuated, or so it is imagined, of history, politics, and indeed nature (a point I pick up again in what follows). Defoe's littoral imprint is cryptic in a manner that chimes with Jodey Castricano's account of a ghostly writing, for 'it stands on the border of divulging *and* hiding, remembering *and* forgetting, producing a curious *fort*/*da* tension that is ... always "becoming"' (Castricano 2001: 29). Despite the later appearance of the man Crusoe calls Friday, the question of whose footprint this might be is never satisfactorily resolved: a haunting remainder of the past, even after the image of the foot has long since been washed away by the incoming tide, which cannot be wholly reconciled to the narrative present.

Crusoe's footprint transforms Defoe's text into something akin to a seaside ghost story, whose spectres speak foremost to the prospect of sovereignty, colonial power, and tyranny (as much over narrative as over territory): 'who is this who has been here before us?' we might ask, in imitation of M. R. James' haunted beachgoer, Professor Parkins. The ghost story, as David Punter defines it, 'never leaves us with [a] sense of a re-established certainty; on the contrary, it reminds us that the story can never be fully told, or re-told, in the present: what "remains" in the present is only ever, indeed, a narrative of remains' (Punter 2016: 38). As I have already suggested, the beach is particularly resistant to any kind of enduring inscription, and is for this reason extremely susceptible to ghostly conjurations. Few stories, we might also note, have been told and re-told as many times as *Robinson Crusoe*. Indeed, the novel's haunting footprint, the frantic speculations over monstrous Others that this impression impels its protagonist to endure, and its eloquent portrait of a haunted shore can be traced through the coastal Gothic tradition.[1] Of the texts under discussion in this Element, for example, Crusoevian encounters with eerie footprints appear in the works of Charlotte Riddell, Bram Stoker, and M. R. James, while the mysterious protagonist of Frances Burney's *The Wanderer* (1814) recasts her perilous experience of escaping the French Revolution and settling on England's southern coast as though she were 'a female Robinson Crusoe, as unaided and unprotected, though in the midst of the world, as that imaginary hero in his uninhabited island' (Burney 1991: 873). However, unlike *Robinson Crusoe*, as Burney hints, these texts are not preoccupied with an 'uninhabited island'; rather, each turns to the Gothic conditions of British and Irish shores and their adjacent waters.

1.2 The Littoral Perspective

My reason for framing this study around a British and Irish coastal Gothic tradition is partly practical. While we might readily identify many national and cultural manifestations of the coastal Gothic, a comprehensive account of this Gothic form is necessarily beyond the scope of any single monograph. And the coastal Gothic of England, Ireland, Scotland, and Wales offers an especially well-established and varied iteration of the genre. Indeed, turning to the haunted shores of Britain and Ireland makes for a productive point of inquiry because, when it comes to the coastlines of these island nations, there are rather a lot of

---

[1] For the importance of 'footfall' to the British and Irish Gothic see also Armitt and Brewster (2022).

them to survey, and they have frequently functioned – and continue to function – in diverse symbolic ways in national imaginaries.

Over 6,000 islands comprise the collection of countries currently known as the United Kingdom and the Republic of Ireland, with over 11,000 miles of coastline around Great Britain and more than 2,000 miles in Ireland (Colley 2014: 13, 23). On these islands, it is extremely difficult to position one's self very far from the shore: it is said that one must travel to Lichfield in the West Midlands to be as far from the coast as possible in the United Kingdom. The difficulty of being free from littoral existence is felt acutely if we tune into the always uncertain and contingent question of where a shoreline, a coast, or a beach might be said to begin and end.[2] As the influential coastal historian John R. Gillis has noted, conceptions of the 'coastline' have 'increasingly given way to the notion of the coastal zone, which can extend hundreds of miles into the interior', with the result that 'It sometimes seems as if Britain is nothing but its coasts' (Gillis 2012: 161). Taking a global perspective, Gillis signals the importance of cultural histories of littoral worlds, arguing that humanity is fundamentally an 'edge species', a dweller on shores (4). It is perhaps for these reasons that W. H. Auden, writing in 1933 from within the shadows of the Malvern Hills (nearly as far from the coast as Lichfield), imagines the decade's political upheavals inundating a moment's pleasure (which is also an inundation of a particular vision of England) in overtly oceanic terms: 'through the dykes of our content/The crumpling flood will force a rent'. Our 'river-dreams' will be devastated by the 'vigours of the sea', carrying 'stranded monsters gasping' far inland and transforming the country into one vast Gothic littoral vista (Auden 2001: 5).

Islandhood, too, has often been a determining factor in articulations of national identities, deriving from the formidable imaginative force that inheres within conceptions of islands.[3] Following the 1707 Act of Union and the formal establishment of the Kingdom of Great Britain, for example, as Linda Colley argues, 'men and women came to define themselves as Britons – in addition to defining themselves in many other ways – because circumstances impressed them with the belief that they were different from those beyond their shores, and in particular different from their prime enemy, the French' (Colley 2003: 17). Robert Tombs puts it rather more boldly at the start of his defence of Britain's 2016 vote to leave the European Union ('Brexit') when he opines that 'Geography comes before history. Islands cannot have the same history as continental plains' (Tombs 2021: 1). Islandhood is seen to be peculiarly well placed for fostering national or

---

[2] On this point see also Richter and Kluwick (2016: 2–3).
[3] The imaginative power of islands is discussed at length by Gillis (2004).

cultural identities rooted in isolation and insularity (and, as one often sees, *exceptionalism*), and which also maintain a suggestively ambivalent relationship with the prospect of foreign invasion: islandhood, being dominated by coastal borders, is both an effective barrier against invasion and a precarious, because easily broached, bulwark.

Histories of British – or, more usually, *English* – nationhood and identity frequently turn on a narrative of audacious (if not always triumphant) resistance to a tidal wave of invasion. England's 'insularity', notes Tombs in fairly pointed language, 'had to be won the hard way . . ., sealed by Nelson at Trafalgar in 1805 . . . . Until Nelson's time, the islands' history was one of innumerable raids and invasions, at least nine of which since the Norman Conquest have overthrown governments' (2). The rhetoric of invasion is also deployed, in obviously hostile terms, in relation to immigration, and narratives of littoral landings are fundamental to many refugee and migrant experiences. As Virginia Richter and Ursula Kluwick outline, 'migrants taking the sea route experience littoral space not as a site of hope and hospitality but, rather, as a non-place', which, 'while part of an international mobility grid, is in fact a place of stasis for those who are not considered legitimate participants in that mobility' (Richter and Kluwick 2016: 12). Globally, images of beaches, unseaworthy boats, and the bodies of migrants caught either dead or alive in littoral space, shape contemporary and historical discourses that stress either the notion of a migration *crisis* or the failures of states to accommodate and treat with humanity those seeking asylum.[4]

Nor is the significance of the coast to British and Irish Gothic literature simply explicable via ambivalent relationships with the European mainland and further afield. Archipelagic interconnections – movements between the coasts of England, Ireland, Scotland, and Wales – are just as significant to the coastal Gothic and the senses of identity interrogated therein. The rise of Gothic literature is roughly coeval with the rise of the coastal resort and seaside vacation, whose origins sit in the mid eighteenth century, with the development of health resorts which gradually, over the course of the nineteenth century, transformed into sites of pleasure and recreation (Corbin 1994 and Walton 1983). By the early twentieth century, as John K. Walton notes, 'Britain, and England in particular, had a system of coastal resorts whose scale and complexity was unmatched anywhere else in the world' (Walton 2000: 27). Walton's account of the poetics and politics of the seaside has a distinctly Gothic resonance:

> The seaside puts the 'civilising process' temporarily into reverse … and conjures up the spirit of carnival, in the sense of upturning the social order and

---
[4] On the littoral in Mediterranean migration narratives see Caserta (2022).

> celebrating the rude, the excessive, the anarchic, the hidden and the gross, in ways which generate tension and put respectability on the defensive[.] (4)

The beach is a site of spectacle and exhibition(ism), a world in which otherwise pervasive forms of social distinction or segregation *supposedly* come undone. For these reasons, as we see in Section 2, uneasy and uncanny encounters readily transpire along the shorelines of the British-Irish archipelago.

For John Brannigan, the archipelagic perspective also offers a valuable counterpart to the unionising and anti-unionist efforts that have shaped the history of this north Atlantic archipelago for several hundred years. To read the literature of this region 'archipelagically', and situate water rather than land at the heart of questions of identity and affiliation, is to consider 'a plural and connective vision quite at odds with the cultural and political homogenisation which lay at the heart of the Unionist project' and 'at odds with the nationalist project which, largely in reaction to Unionism, cherished exceptionalism and insularity' (Brannigan 2015: 6). For Brannigan, 'the social and cultural connections of the people who live in the archipelago always exceed the limits of state or national formations' (10). The coast and the archipelago, and the 'many moments of transition between land and sea that occur in Irish literature', are also crucial to Nicholas Allen's recent study of Irish writing from the nineteenth century to the present (Allen 2021: 4). Allen not only highlights the 'significant transoceanic contexts' (12) that shape Irish-British relations over this period, but identifies an ambivalent affect that shades literary engagements with littoral space:

> From dampness to drownings, many of the writers have taken the coast as a zone of continuing sadness. This is a tidal margin that never quite recedes to catastrophe and never rises to happiness; caught in the middle, it is a literature of dreams, disquiet and habitual accommodation. (16)

In terms especially resonant with this Element, Allen speaks of Irish coastal literature as 'both haunted and epiphanic' (15). This is a compelling prospect, and, as we have already started to see via *Robinson Crusoe*, a coastal Gothic imaginary could be said to elide the distinction between these terms: we will see more than once across the following sections numerous littoral epiphanies that are prompted by, and themselves come to be, *haunting*.

Before turning to the detailed case studies that begin in Section 2, I want to use the remainder of this Introduction to further sketch out some of the defining characteristics of a coastal Gothic poetics. Following this, Section 2 examines coastal Gothic narratives of intra-archipelagic travel and the Gothic seaside vacation. In Section 3, I focus on the role of war and invasion in coastal Gothic writing. Section 4 considers Gothic figurations of migrant and refugee narratives, with a particular focus on uncanny littoral encounters. And Section 5 offers a brief conclusion via a key architectural feature of the coastal Gothic: the lighthouse, which I place in dialogue with the Gothic castle.

1.3 Beyond the Pleasure Beach

Among the authors of Romantic-era Gothic, Ann Radcliffe evidences the most sustained and complex fascination with coasts. Her fiction is saturated with coastal episodes and short embedded verses that often speak to the symbolic valences of littoral zones. Of particular importance to Radcliffe's works is the imbrication of typical Gothic edifices within precarious coastal terrain and coastal waters. At the start of her first novel, for example, we are told that the Castle of Athlin, located on Scotland's north-east coast, is 'an edifice built on the summit of a rock whose base was in the sea' (Radcliffe 1995: 3), and the strange interconnection between coastal landscapes and subterranean vaults finds its most elegant expression in the latter half of *A Sicilian Romance* (1790), where it remains difficult to pinpoint quite where the coast ends and the castle's tomb-like labyrinth begins. The coast exerts a powerful agency over the Gothic plot in Radcliffe's fiction: it is frequently a site of peculiar transportation, literally and metaphysically. As Joan Passey argues, the coast for Radcliffe is 'a liminal threshold – a space between life and death, a portal unto the fantastical, and imaginative gap ripe for terrific reflection' (Passey 2021: 131–132). Radcliffe's attentiveness to coastal spaces also forms a major part of the personal writings excerpted by Thomas Noon Talfourd in the memoir attached to Radcliffe's posthumously published final novel, *Gaston de Blondeville* (1826).

A trip along the Kent coast in 1797 provides Radcliffe with an opportunity to reflect on international violence and Britain's involvement in the French Revolutionary Wars (1792–1802). On 3 September, for example, Radcliffe writes that she 'Walked on the beach, watching the retiring and returning waves, and attending to the bursting thunder of the surge'; later she surveys 'a vast marine horizon, with a long tract of the French coast, a white line bounding the blue waters' (Talfourd 1826: 19). As Angela Wright has previously shown, Radcliffe's careful attentiveness to unsettled coastal atmospherics and a visible French presence 'hint[s] at despair with the ever-worsening conflict that Radcliffe finds difficult to articulate' (Wright 2013: 112). At such moments, the coast is a threshold, though perhaps not wholly a liminal one, offering privileged access to the wider world of political turmoil in which the writer's home nation is implicated. Radcliffe also speaks of the rugged coastline in a recognisably Gothic tenor following a later excursion to the cliffs of Beachy

Head in East Sussex – a popular tourist destination and, more notoriously, a common site for suicides, a reputation it would already have had in the 1790s and which necessarily shadows Radcliffe's writing (and Charlotte Smith's more famous 1807 poem named for the cliffs).

In her writing on Beachy Head, Radcliffe emphasises the ruinous sublimity of the scene, suggesting that the coast is an especially inviting site for the Gothic author as it exhibits a form of natural ruination that is usually the preserve of the artificial stonework in castles and abbeys:

> Almost frightened at the solitude and vastness of the scene though *Chance* was with me. Tide almost out; only sea in front; white cliffs rising over me, but not impending; strand all around a chaos of rocks and fallen cliffs, far out into the waves; sea-fowl wheeling and screaming; all disappeared behind the point, beyond which, is the great cliff; but we had doubled point after point, in the hope that this would be the next, and had been much deceived in the distances by these great objects . . . . Slowly and laboriously we made our way back along the beach, greatly fatigued, the day exceedingly hot, the horizon sulphurous, with lowering clouds; thunder rolled faintly at a distance. (Talfourd 1826: 41–42)

This Gothic vision of cliffs and shoreline builds to an almost apocalyptic sense of the 'sulphurous' shorescape. Part of the Gothic affect of this passage – which has less to do with terror or horror than a kind of intense vexation – originates in the difficulties that attend surmounting the littoral terrain: rocks impede the way and the shoreline extends interminably onwards, forever promising but thwarting an arrival at the desired 'great cliff'. Time and space are stretched at the shore, as endings are intimated and deferred, impressing the individual with a desolate isolation (despite the reassuring companionship of a dog like Chance). Radcliffe's prose, here, too, seeks to accommodate the ruinous fragmentation characterising this crumbling shorescape: the desolate coast is *felt* through Radcliffe's disjointed syntax and the staccato rhythm of short observations that are held tentatively and precariously together via repeated semicolons. We stumble slowly through Radcliffe's writing, as she makes slow headway along the shore.

The environmental precarity that Radcliffe perceives along England's southern shoreline is given further Gothic expression in the poetry of Charlotte Smith. Smith's poetry shows a keen attentiveness to the multiple and overlapping connotations associated with the English coast, particularly the south coast of Sussex. The coast is a rich palimpsest of history, especially histories of foreign invasion (as exemplified in *Beachy Head* [1807]), yet it can offer respite from the terrors of the contemporary moment (as in *The Emigrants* [1793]); yet, again, the sea's edge is a site for loners and castaways, as in the courageous hermit we encounter in the final lines of *Beachy Head* or the 'lunatic' who frequents 'Sonnet LXX' (1797). Smith reserves her most luridly Gothic accounts of the coast, however, for those sonnets dealing with the burial (and unburial) of the dead in littoral ground. In these sonnets, the sea churns violently against the fragile beaches and disintegrating chalk cliffs of southern England, pulling the country – and the restless dead – piece by piece into the ocean's depths. Such horrors inform Smith's most gruesome coastal poem, 'Sonnet XLIV' (1789). Set, as the headnote tells us, in a churchyard in Middleton, Sussex, the sonnet tells a ghastly tale of corpses cascading into the sea due to coastal erosion:

> Press'd by the Moon, mute arbitress of tides,
>> While the loud equinox its power combines,
>> The sea no more its swelling surge confines,
> But o'er the shrinking land sublimely rides.
> The wild blast, rising from the Western cave,
>> Drives the huge billows from their heaving bed;
>> Tears from their grassy tombs the village dead,
> And breaks the silent sabbath of the grave!
> With shells and sea-weed mingled, on the shore
>> Lo! their bones whiten in the frequent wave[.] (Smith 2017: 85)

A grisly note appended to the poem by Smith explains that the encroachment of the sea on Middleton means that the local graveyard's wall 'is entirely swept away, many of the graves broken up, and the remains of bodies interred washed into the sea: whence human bones are found among the sand and shingles on the shore' (85).

As Smith – and Middleton's population – knows, coasts are not stable spaces, and they are unlikely ever to have the same appearance from one day to the next: part of the Gothic appeal of the coastline has to do with this unsettlement and the sense that, because of erosion, coasts *move inland*, imbuing *terra firma* with the terror of instability. Further, the commingling of corpses with 'shells and sea-weed' evocatively portrays the manner in which human integrity is as much imperilled by coastal erosion as the land on which we live (and in which we may be buried): Smith's poem, in this respect, looks ahead to M. R. James' 'A Warning to the Curious' (1925), with its climactic image of the violent intermingling of human bone and shingle. In turn, both texts remind us of the simple fact that beaches themselves are sometimes composed of organic skeletal fragments; this is particularly so of tropical beaches, whose desirable white sands have thanatic origins.

Smith's poems also remind us of the role that sea-burial itself might play in coastal Gothic imaginaries. Taking a short voyage west from the Sussex coast brings you to The Needles, off the coast of the Isle of Wight, one of the few places in the United Kingdom where sea-burials are permitted (Marine Management Organisation 2024). While the location supposedly ensures the safe disposal of human remains, bodies have a history of washing ashore again. The return of the dead has been such a problem on the Isle of Wight in recent years that the island's former Conservative MP, Bob Seely, has successfully campaigned for new regulations regarding burial at The Needles. Seely spoke in distinctly Gothic terms in a Parliamentary debate in October 2021, emphasising the horrors of the dead returning to shore and the need for firmer regulatory guidelines: 'In October, a headless torso was found at Brook chine. In 2018, a skeleton was found on Barton beach and a skull was found in St Helens, with another being found later in the year in Seaview'. These washings ashore are most likely to occur after storms, 'which either break up a coffin or force a body on to the land'; remains are then 'often discovered by dog walkers on the beaches, and that is clearly not the sort of thing that they want to see first thing in the morning' ('Judicial Review' 2021). Seely's words portray life on the Isle of Wight as inflected by some very Gothic beachcombing, whereby beachgoers find themselves stumbling upon, and sharing littoral terrain with, the dead.

From the perspectives outlined so far, littoral space is not so much a Gothic site of death and disaster – though this is important, as we see in the famous shipwreck sequence in Charles Maturin's *Melmoth the Wanderer* (1820). Instead, the littoral environment is a potent site of Gothic unburials. These unburials might be haunting because they are unexpected, as in the case of Smith's poetry. But the coast is also a site receptive to the *intentional* unearthing of objects and bodies that have been interred in the soft pliable sands and fragile rock of the coast. Identifying the seaside as somewhere shaped by 'elaborate sequence[s] of rituals', Alexandra Harris reads in Elizabeth Bowen's *The Little Girls* (1964) a suggestively Gothic streak, with characters 'obsessively burying and unearthing strange objects in the thickets along the coast' (Harris 2009: 227, 237). Obsessive acts of burial and unburial are vital to the Gothic tradition, coastal or otherwise. They find their greatest littoral expression in the short fiction of M. R. James. In 'Oh, Whistle, and I'll Come to You, My Lad' (1904) and 'A Warning to the Curious', that which is unburied speaks explicitly to national histories and the long, haunting legacy of international conflict: the whistle in the vicinity of the Templar's preceptory and a Saxon crown buried to ward off foreign invasion, respectively. These buried objects call attention to efforts aimed at shoring up the integrity and safety of the nation from threatening Others; their unburial thus necessarily precipitates an existential crisis for James' unfortunate excavators.

The ecotonal qualities and the tidal ebb and flow of coastal worlds suit a Gothic preoccupation with the unsettlement of buried matter and uncanny returns. Indeed, as we've already seen, the coast is a site where the ground itself is hauntingly unstill. Moving beyond the imperilled southern coast of England discussed thus far, we might head further north, to the tidal causeway surrounding Eel Marsh House in Susan Hill's *The Woman in Black* (1983) – a novel in explicit dialogue with James' coastal Gothic – in order to think about unsettlement and unburial in the context of a littoral landscape that is not crumbling and fragmented, but dank and oozy, continuously inundated by the tides and rendered swamp-like. Hill's novel repeatedly emphasises the treacherous nature of the quicksand and marshland characterising Nine Lives Causeway, a topographical feature isolating Eel Marsh House from the rest of its local community. Hill's portrayal of this inundated landscape might be glossed via remarks made by Lowell Duckert on the cultural conception of swampland as 'danger zone[s], areas of interstitial terror, the spatial borders of civilized development that somehow fan out and hem in at the same time': 'The sphagnous sucks away stability, empties the illusion of solid ground, darkens the elusive transparent' (Duckert 2017: 205, 207). The causeway is a site of engulfment, whose submerged terrors and tragedies destabilise Kipps' otherwise rather dry labours: the swamp, to quote Steve Mentz, 'hides interruptions beneath the water', exhibiting a 'disorienting pull and voyage-stopping suction' (Mentz 2013: 195, 199).

Indeed, *Woman in Black* presents its littoral ooze as a Gothic counterpart to the more mundane papers and archives that occupy large portions of the narrative. For if the coast is a potent site of unburial, it also functions evocatively as a kind of archive, one where history has been 'voyage-stopp[ed]', and which must be entered into, sifted through, in order to bring its histories to light. Such terrain is interstitial in profoundly Gothic terms: it is not soil, into which bodies and histories rot and decay, nor is it water, in which bodies might dissolve and dissipate, but a preservative in which our pasts and their horrors may endure. Thus, the piteous cries of a drowned boy – the novel's pivotal horror – speak from a state of unresolved suspension. Here is just one moment Kipps encounters this voice, after 'a thick, damp sea-mist' has rolled in 'over the marshes and enveloped everything' (Hill 2016: 85):

> The noise of the pony trap grew fainter and then stopped abruptly and away on the marsh was a curious draining, sucking, churning sound, which went on, together with the shrill neighing and whinnying of a horse in panic, and then I heard another cry, a shout, a terrified sobbing – it was hard to decipher – but with horror I realized that it came from a child, a young child. (87–88)

It is clear that Hill's littoral spaces are foremost haunting at the level of sound rather than sight, productive of epistemological uncertainty: Kipps presumes the horror is unfurling in his present, rather than emanating from the past. Hill's prose can also be productively compared with Radcliffe's. Where Radcliffe's rock-strewn coast produces clipped and fragmented syntax, Hill's causeway occasions distinctly oozy sentence structures. Throughout *Woman in Black*, Hill's affect-laden sentences wrap clause into clause, the train of thought oozing along, reflecting the mire. One final point to make here has to do with the effect these oozy encounters have on the living humans who have to contend with them. Early in Hill's story, we learn that the marshes cannot be 'drained to any purpose' (62). Kipps also emphasises the 'draining' sound the marsh makes in the passage previously quoted. The causeway cannot *be* drained, but it *is* draining. 'On reading Mrs Drablow's papers', says Kipps, 'I felt drained, exhausted' (150); later, too, he is 'exhausted, drained, but well' (190). If the littoral world cannot be drained and continues to conceal things within it, the people who encounter it nonetheless find themselves evacuated of something: the oozy world drains them.

The final form of littoral terrain I want to touch on in this Introduction is perhaps the most cherished among the majority of visitors to the shore: the coastal promenades and fine sands of the seaside town. A succinct example of the seaside Gothic can be found in the short story 'Seashore Macabre: A Moment's Experience' (1933) by Hugh Walpole (a distant relative of Horace Walpole). In 'Seashore Macabre', the narrator recalls a brief episode from his youth, when, during a family holiday to the town of Seascale, he obeys a mysterious impulse to follow a man from the town's shops to a small beach hut. Here, he sees two people and, on a table, a corpse (all of whom may, in fact, be distinct iterations of the *same* person, prophetic visions even of the narrator himself). Suddenly, the wind whips up and 'everything spr[ings] to life':

> The room was filled with the wind. Sand came blowing in. Everything was on the move; it seemed to me that the yellow-faced corpse raised his hand . . .
> Screaming, I ran for my life [. . .]. A moment's experience – yes, but Mr. Freud might say – a lifetime's consequence. (Walpole 2016: 102)

The tale playfully cajoles us into a psychoanalytical reading of events, where the libidinal pleasures and temptations towards exhibitionism historically inflecting English beach culture are a gateway to an uncanny encounter with 'the utmost of abjection' (Kristeva 1982: 4) – namely, the corpse that lives and that mocks the nascent psychosexual development of the child. But the story's several knowing allusions to Freud, made with a nod and a wink, pre-empt and undercut this.

Instead, as a Gothic tale of an identity crisis, the proper subject of 'Seashore Macabre' is not the young boy but the town itself. The eerily animate corpse on the beach makes most sense as an embodiment of the living death into which Seascale will be plunged. Seascale, the narrator tells us, appeared, in his youth, 'as though one day it might become a true resort': 'It had long, lazy sands, a new golf course, a fine hotel, and there were little roads and lanes in and about that looked as though, with the slightest encouragement, they might become quite busy shop-haunted streets'; yet 'Seascale has never taken that step upward into commercial prosperity that once perhaps was hoped for it' (Walpole 2016: 98). Walpole's short story offers another vision of Gothicised littoral suspension. The seaside has become 'shop-haunted', but not quite in the way one might have hoped: the town has ossified, a reminder of the once-prosperous nature of the English seaside holiday.

1.4 Against Liminality

Outside the Gothic tradition, few writers have limned the ecology of the coast as wonderfully as the US writer Rachel Carson, who envisions the scientific realities of littoral zones as constantly rubbing alongside cryptic and occult perceptions of the shoreline's meaning, whose 'elusiveness ... haunts us' (Carson 2021: 8). Indeed, Carson's portrait of the New England coast in *The Edge of the Sea* (1955) culminates with a moment of astonishing transcendence. She observes how

> The restive waters, the cold wet breath of the fog, are of a world in which man is an uneasy trespasser; ... these coastal forms merge and blend in a shifting, kaleidoscopic pattern in which there is no finality, no ultimate and fixed reality – earth becoming fluid as the sea itself. On all these shores there are echoes of past and future: of the flow of time, obliterating yet containing all that has gone before. ... Contemplating the teeming life of the shore, we have an uneasy sense of the communication of some universal truth that lies just beyond our grasp . ... The meaning haunts and ever eludes us, and in its very pursuit we approach the ultimate mystery of Life itself. (279–280)

The shimmering opacity of Carson's coast unfolds in a literary register akin to modernist poetry – recalling T. S. Eliot's 'The Dry Salvages' (1941), where a New England beach 'hints of earlier and other creation' (Eliot 1974: 192). Much could be made of the role of haunting, the hauntingly epiphanic, and transgression in the littoral imaginations of these writers. But Carson's attention to 'the teeming life' of the littoral ecotone alerts us to another quality of the coast that I argue the Gothic similarly energetically celebrates. In popular and scholarly cultures, littoral zones are overwhelmingly commonly framed as liminal worlds, and as spaces that produce forms of existential liminality in those who deign to dwell on such an unsteady edge. One of the paramount contributions I hope to make with this Element – to Gothic studies and to coastal studies and the blue humanities – is a sense of the value of resisting the urge to read the coast too readily through a lens of liminality.

A guiding principle in this Element is that coasts are edges, but they are not (always) liminal. My approach here is akin to the imperatives shaping archipelagic studies, which make oceanic space the central figure in 'our sea[s] of islands' (to adopt Epeli Hau'ofa's influential coinage (Hau'ofa 2008: 27–40)). As I hope to show across the following sections, as a Gothic topography, and as political, cultural, and social environments ripe with Gothic potential, coasts are *central*; they are centre-points in the articulation of national and individual identities. Liminality matters, of course, but foremost as a topic whose scrutiny helps us better understand how coasts have long been imagined – as a sign of the readiness by which coastal imaginaries travel in Gothic directions. As William Hughes affirms in his discussion of Gothic regionalism:

> the Gothic is uniquely and consistently concerned with liminal and transitional states and, by the logical necessity of definition, such states require a functional centre against which to balance their epistemological Otherness. The negotiations between centre and margin in Gothic, however, are seldom so convenient as to permit their being rationalised as simple binaries. (Hughes 2018: 1)

Coastal Gothic offers a rich seam of material for the study of the Gothic's complex relationship with regionality. At the Gothic coast centre and margin, the metropolitan and the provincial, insider and outsider, self and Other, jostle powerfully and uneasily beside one another. The particular topographies of the shorescape, as outlined in this Introduction, provide a valuable stage for ritualised and dramatic encounters with national and cultural limit-points, for the unsettlement or erasure of abiding senses of identity, for obscure and abrupt departures, and cryptic and marvellous arrivals.

2 Archipelagic Gothic and the Seaside

Matthew Arnold begins *On the Study of Celtic Literature* (1867) – the published version of four lectures given in 1865 – with a vision of the colonisation by English holidaymakers of Llandudno, a town on Wales' northern coast, in which Arnold himself had recently holidayed. 'The best lodging-houses at Llandudno', Arnold observes, 'look eastward, towards Liverpool; and from that Saxon hive swarms are incessantly issuing, crossing the bay, and taking possession of the beach and the lodging-houses' (Arnold 1867: 1). Arnold's essay offers a colonial and exoticised view of the so-called "Celtic fringe", lamenting the enduring peripherality of Celtic culture unless there is an imminent 'fusion of all the inhabitants of these islands into one homogenous, English-speaking whole' (12). By abandoning supposedly obsolete languages, and appointing 'a chair of Celtic at Oxford' (178), who can offer a scholarly appraisal of the influence of Celtic cultures on English literature (from the comforts of an English metropole), the 'true unity' of 'these small islands' may (finally) be achieved (xiii).

Arnold's lectures participate in the long and ongoing history of, to adopt Linda Colley's formulation, acts of union and disunion between Cornwall, England, Ireland, Scotland, and Wales (Colley 2014). In Jarlath Killeen's evocative words, Arnold's proposed 'programme for peace' is akin to the Gothic horrors perpetrated by H. G. Wells' Doctor Moreau, who 'is trying to graft on to beasts the minds of rational Englishmen, just as Arnold advocated a grafting of the English mind on to the exotic body of Celtic subordinates' (Killeen 2009: 105). And just as Wells isolates his mad doctor on a small island, so too does Arnold approach his subject by emphasising islandhood (frequently a means, as previously noted, for concocting unity) and contested shorelines.[5] Arnold's opening remarks highlight the seaside holiday as making especially visible England's onslaught on the society of its nearest neighbours, because of the desirability of that littoral zone – an onslaught that is ongoing, as owners of second homes and tourist lets run roughshod over local housing markets in attractive seaside settings. Taking Arnold as its point of departure, this section is interested in coastal Gothic narratives that examine the uncanny cultures localised in particular coastal communities and that foreground the archipelagic relationships between England, Ireland, Scotland, and Wales, via stories that portray citizens of one of these nations (usually England) visiting or occupying the shores of another. The section thus interrogates the tensions that are registered between the coast's permanent local inhabitants and visitors; this is in turn to explore conflicts between national and localised senses of identity. I draw in particular on the work of Elizabeth Gaskell, Charlotte Riddell, Bram Stoker, and Robert Aickman.

2.1 Gaskell, Doom, and the Vasty Deep

In her discussion of Gaskell's development of a northern Gothic regionalist mode, Catherine Spooner has argued that 'Gaskell's attempt to capture the local

---

[5] The importance of the coast for Arnold as a site for uneasy reflections on the state of the nation is also evident in his most famous poem, 'Dover Beach', published the same year as his *Study of Celtic Literature*.

environment not only in terms of its physical features but also the legends and stories inhering in a place . . . provides a kind of nascent rural psychogeography' (Spooner 2018: 35). Local folklore, Spooner indicates, is the 'driving force of many of [Gaskell's] Gothic tales' (36). This holds true, for the most part, for Gaskell's Welsh Gothic tale, 'The Doom of the Griffiths' (1858), a narrative propelled by the playing out of a legendary curse. But the coastal setting of Gaskell's 'Doom' also begins to unsettle the extent to which things might *inhere* in a 'tract of land' that seems to have 'been redeemed at no distant period of time from the sea' and which exhibits 'the desolate rankness often attendant upon such marshes' (Gaskell 2000: 105). The story is set on Wales' north-west coast[6] and tells of the extinction of the male line of the Griffiths family, having been cursed generations previously by the Welsh folk hero Owain Glyndŵr following an act of betrayal. Gaskell's narrative culminates in a series of violent deaths and disappearances into coastal waters, as Squire Robert Griffiths inadvertently kills his grandson while reprimanding his son, Owen, for marrying below his station; Owen then inadvertently kills his father, the Squire. With the aid of his father-in-law, Owen and his wife, Nest, flee the ancestral home, Bodowen, by heading out to sea, never to be seen again. I want first to briefly outline Gaskell's Gothic portrait of the Welsh coast before turning to reflect on the recessive but significant English presence in Gaskell's framing remarks and the coast's role in performing cultural erasure.

Gaskell gives us a distinctly ecoGothic figuration of Cardigan Bay and the vicinity of Criccieth: it is 'dark and overhung by sea-fog' (105), constituted by dank, wet earth, and a dangerously rocky coastline. The instability and precarity defining this littoral world become productive of epistemic and ontological unsettlement: the coast is not simply a zone of unsure footing, but a zone precipitating other forms of uncertainty. When the Squire falls to his death in the waters of the bay, Owen swiftly hides his father's body in his boat. Yet Owen, panicking, struggles to assure himself of his father's death. He repeatedly gazes back into the boat 'to see if there had been any movement of life': 'It was all quiet deep down below, but as he gazed the shifting light gave the appearance of a slight movement'; still, fearful of 'leaving his father unaided while yet a spark of life lingered – he removed the shrouding cover. The eyes looked into his with a dead stare!' (132). Despite the uncanny vitality that briefly manifests within the Squire's corpse (he is dead but the eyes 'stare!'), it is the coastal environment that imparts animacy: the gently rocking boat coupled with the dappling light playing over the makeshift sailcloth shroud suggests the slow ebbing and flowing of life. A little later, Owen returns to convey the body

---

[6] On Gaskell's familiarity with this region see Uglow (1993: 49–52, 122–125, 187–188).

for secret burial on a small island (Bardsey Island) just off the Llŷn Peninsula, but the boat has gone: 'It had broken loose and disappeared' (137).

Elsewhere in this Element, I am interested in the coast as a site of uncanny returns. But here there is no return – though the threat of it remains ever present – and Gaskell's Welsh coast is really a zone of uncanny disappearances. Unlike the oozy marshland of *Woman in Black*, which functions as an accessible archive to the region's horrors, the coastal waters of 'Doom' provide no means of recovering what is lost. This would seem to be quite convenient for Owen, except that the body *may yet* be washed ashore: Gaskell's Gothic terrors lie foremost in this condition of uncertainty. A similar doom to that afflicting the Squire's corpse awaits Owen and Nest. In the tale's final lines, we are told:

> It was absolutely necessary that they should leave the country for a time. Through those stormy waters they must plough their way that very night. . . . They sailed into the tossing darkness, and were never more seen of men.
>
> The house of Bodowen has sunk into damp, dark ruins; and a Saxon stranger holds the lands of the Griffiths. (138)

The unresolved fate of Owen and Nest echoes the more famous conclusion of Mary Shelley's *Frankenstein* (1818), as the creature escapes across a littoral zone of Arctic ice, becoming 'lost in darkness and distance', ambiguously committed to his promise of self-immolation (Shelley 1999: 244).[7]

More pertinent, however, for its archipelagic politics is the text's concluding sentence. Bodowen has been transformed into a site of coastal Gothic ruin – itself 'sunk', like so many of its former inhabitants may be, into the littoral environment – and this territory is now held by 'a Saxon stranger'. This terminology resonates with Arnold's language, which portrays Liverpool as a 'Saxon hive' from which 'swarms are incessantly issuing'. (Liverpool, as it happens, is also the city into which Owen and Nest anticipate hiding themselves, for there 'no one will know where you are' (Gaskell 2000: 136).) The opening of Gaskell's story, too, strangely chimes with Arnold, for Gaskell's narrator begins by outlining the story of Owain Glyndŵr, noting that he was 'the subject of the Welsh prize poem at Oxford, some fifteen or sixteen years ago' – 'the most proudly national subject that had been given for years' (103). Here, as well, the narrator struggles to find a space for a Welsh voice: recounting Glyndŵr's magical powers, we are told that 'He says himself – or Shakespeare says it for him, which is much the same thing – ... "I can call spirits from the vasty deep"' (103). The English Shakespeare, depicting

---

[7] We can also hear in Gaskell's words a version of the final lines of *Paradise Lost* (1667/1674), as Owen and Nest endure their sudden expulsion from their Edenic idyll and must confront the world at large.

Glyndŵr in *1 Henry IV* (c.1597),[8] stands in as an authentic mouthpiece for the Welsh folk hero.

These framing remarks, foregrounding the otherwise absent English, serve two connected functions in Gaskell's coastal Gothic story. First, they establish the narrative's archipelagic perspective, suggesting that this is not (or not only) a tale about internecine Welsh conflict. The narrative voice is fundamentally English, telling a tale of Welsh factionalism and the cursed histories that play out in the supposedly peripheral and provincial regions of the United Kingdom. Second, this factionalism is framed as something that (literally) clears the way for English possession of Welsh territory: Owen and Nest never make the anticipated return to their homeland, and the 'Saxon stranger' easily takes 'possession of the beach and the lodging-houses' (to recall Arnold) when the Welsh gentry have cast themselves into the Irish Sea. Indeed, Gaskell's archipelagic journeys work in distinctly Gothic terms, as the movement is eerily unidirectional: her Welsh characters voyage into oblivion when they try to move from periphery to centre (they 'were never more seen of men'), while the English are readily able to co-opt Welsh national myths and Welsh soil. In this respect, Gaskell's quotation from *1 Henry IV* is telling. If any 'spirits' are summoned over the course of this Gothic curse narrative, it is the spectral (and, as it were, peripheral) English; what Glyndŵr's curse in fact achieves is a committing of spirits *into* the vasty deep, a drowning of Welsh heritage in coastal waters and dispossession of territory. The suggestion of a fatal covenant and obliviating submersion in the ocean also sits at the heart of Charles Maturin's and Charlotte Riddell's Irish Gothic fiction.

2.2 Strangers on the Shore in Maturin and Riddell

Haunted shores and seas play an important role in Irish Gothic imaginaries. Irish narratives of the Irish Sea, Claire Connolly writes, 'understand the waters between Ireland and Britain as fomented by violent conflicts', often associated with the English occupation and colonisation of Ireland and the fraught legacies this history bequeathed to both national and localised forms of identity (Connolly 2020: 243). Connolly, for example, highlights the suggestively Gothic legend that the body of Oliver Cromwell, who led the 1649 invasion of Ireland, was thrown into the Irish Sea after the earth refused his corpse, and thus the waters have been 'very turbulent ever since' (243).[9] Canonical Gothic literature, too, turns to the Irish coast in order to offer reflections on distinctly national and political concerns.

---

[8] See Shakespeare (1987: 3.1.51).

[9] This account of Cromwell's body is one of several legends implying that the corpse of England's republican figurehead functions as an enduring force of unsettlement even as it becomes unlocatable.

Charles Maturin's *Melmoth the Wanderer* uses the treacherous and storm-swept shoreline as a way to think back to English colonial enterprises. The Melmoth family are explicitly framed as colonists, as the first Melmoth in Ireland was 'an officer in Cromwell's army, who obtained a grant of lands, the confiscated property of an Irish family' (Maturin 2012: 24). Two chapters later a storm begins battering the Irish coast and the novel's narrator, John, reminds us that 'Terror is very fond of associations', providing as evidence the symbolic import of a 'tremendous storm that shook all England on the night of Cromwell's death' (70). John himself is briefly thrown into 'the roaring deep' and 'engulphed' (76) after being overwhelmed by the spectacle of a shipwreck and through his exertions in trying to reach the wanderer, who is seen scornfully mocking the disaster. Here, Maturin allusively connects the death-dealing terror of the tempestuous coastline with Ireland's colonial history and a legacy of English dispossession and violence.[10] Though there is no explicit reason to think about someone like Cromwell – 'the odious demon from across the sea' (Covington 2013) – during the shipwreck sequence, the coastal violence nonetheless draws John's (and Maturin's) thinking in this direction, shadowed perhaps by the legend of Cromwell's own oceanic interment, which John himself risks duplicating, and which the wanderer *does* duplicate at the novel's end. The coast becomes a site to meditate on other forms of violent incursion, forms which account for the presence of the Melmoths in Ireland in the first place.

Charlotte Riddell's Gothic tales similarly exhibit a preoccupation with Irish-English relations, and they move often between Irish lands and the colonial metropole, a movement reflecting Riddell's own life: she was born in Carrickfergus in County Antrim in 1832 and moved, due to financial pressures, to London in 1855.[11] For Riddell, the Irish coast has an especially significant function as an historical zone of Irish-English confrontation. And in a similar vein to Gaskell's 'Doom', Riddell's coastal Gothic portrays the meeting point between land and sea as a space of cultural loss and erasure: 'a zone of continuing sadness', to recall Nicholas Allen's words. Riddell's most focused interrogation of the coast as a site of oblivion and strange, supernatural encounters can be found in her short story 'The Last of Squire Ennismore' (1888), set on Ireland's west coast in the fictional Ardwinsagh Bay. Echoing Gaskell, this is a tale in large part about the destruction the Irish aristocracy might bring upon

---

[10] This allusiveness of representation might also be identified in *Frankenstein*: Jarlath Killeen argues that the discovery of Henry Clerval's corpse on the Irish coast in Shelley's novel 'should be read as an occluded representation of the 1798 rebellion' – when Irish and French forces took arms against the British occupiers (Killeen 2014: 5).

[11] For a biographical sketch of Riddell see Dawson (2022).

itself: the story concerns the mysterious death of the decadent Squire Ennismore who, sometime after claiming a puncheon of brandy from among the wreckage of a ship on his stretch of coastline, is last seen walking into the ocean in the company of a peculiar figure who is quite probably the devil.[12] But this is a tale once more framed around an English presence, for the narrative is being told by a local for the entertainment of someone identified only as 'the Englishman', whose landlord has previously refused to rehearse the story because 'the whole rigmarole was nonsense, put together to please strangers' (Riddell 1888: 222, 221). What it might mean to 'please strangers', and what a 'stranger' on the shore might connote, are considerations at the heart of the coastal politics of this Gothic tale.

Following in *Crusoe*'s footstep, Riddell's short story is intensely invested in the multitude of Gothic connotations that inhere within an encounter at the shoreline with a 'stranger', a word that recurs insistently across the few pages of 'Squire Ennismore'. Above all, the word applies to the unknown individual who eventually conveys the Squire to his watery doom. Apparently a survivor of the wreck of the notably 'foreign vessel' (226) that goes to pieces on the headland, the figure is described as 'a stranger who walked the shore alone at night' (227). He was, we are told, 'a dark man, the same colour as the drowned crew lying in the chapel grave-yard' (227), an odd turn of phrase that racialises this figure and the crew from which he is now separated while, at the same time, implying that he is the colour of the *drowned* – an undead littoral wanderer. After several failures to speak with this stranger in English and French, the Squire eventually manages to strike up a friendship when he begins 'speaking a language you'd have thought nobody could understand; but, faith, it seemed natural as kissing to the stranger' (230). When the Squire and the stranger disappear into the ocean together at the tale's end, all that remains in the soft sand of the beach is the devilish 'print of a cloven foot' (233). Beyond this application, the word 'stranger' is used, as we have seen, by the Englishman's landlord: the Gothic legend only exists 'to please strangers'. It is also used in reference to the landlord himself, as the Englishman's Irish interlocutor dismissively says of the landlord: 'what is he but a stranger himself? And how should he know about the doings of real quality like the Ennismores?' (221).

Riddell exploits the rich range of meanings conveyed in the word 'stranger': historically, the term might refer to a foreigner, a newcomer, someone simply unknown to us, someone who is unrelated to us, and, most Gothic of all, the devil. All of these meanings are in play in 'Squire Ennismore', just as many of them are in play in Gaskell's allusion to the 'Saxon stranger' in 'Doom'. From the seaside

---

[12] On the coast as a gateway to hell in Irish Gothic writing see Potter (2022).

holiday to the history of colonial endeavours, the shoreline is a pre-eminent site for encounters with strangers. Moreover, as Riddell's tale details, the littoral world is a zone of estrangement, where one's status as stranger comes to the fore, where a latent condition of 'stranger-ness' becomes a predominating marker of identity – even to those who may well be citizens of the nation, such as the landlord, whose name, Riley, hints at his Irishness. Indeed, the multitude of strangers who occupy Riddell's Irish coast – the devil, the landlord, the English tourist – bear witness to the erosion, or at least displacement, of local presences at the shoreline. Even language itself is imperilled here: the Squire is forced to adopt a linga franca that 'you'd have thought nobody could understand' in order to commune with the stranger. Neither the imposed language of the colonist (English), nor the language of an ally (French) is suitable; could this incomprehensible language, in fact, be Irish Gaelic, indicating a further form of cultural estrangement? Either way, in redolently uncanny terms, these characters themselves 'speak a foreign language' (Freud 2003: 125). The only abiding presence is the Irish narrator, Phil Regan, the repository of local history, carrying, he tells us, the same name as his ancestors (Riddell 1888: 220).

Littoral space is, Riddell's writing declares, a contested zone between competing forms of knowledge and history, a site of dis-integration, where the local gives way to (or is eroded by) external (and infernal) powers. Yet, in the end, this may all be a Gothicised vision of the shoreline devised to 'please strangers'. As the story concludes, the narrator declares that this history is 'true, your honour – every word of it': '"Oh! I have no doubt of that," was the satisfactory reply' from the Englishman (233). Is this 'satisfactory' because the English visitor concedes to the truth of this Gothic narrative, establishing local folklore as a reliable archive of local history? Or does the satisfaction derive from the Englishman's willingness to collude in a piece of touristic hokum? The coastal narrative leaves things indeterminate. The prospect of heading to the coast in order to performatively participate in local and national traditions – with horrifying consequences – is also a paramount concern of Bram Stoker's tale of English holidaymaking and doppelgängers on the Scottish coast, 'Crooken Sands' (1894).

2.3 Stoker, Seaside, and Simulacra

It is perhaps unsurprising that we might meet our Gothic double at the seaside, given the significance of other forms of uncanny simulacrum to the beach as it is often encountered by the holidaying tourist. The beach has a strange unreality about it; it does not quite truly exist. The idealised version of the beach sought after by summer vacationers is founded, writes Jean-Didier Urbain, in 'a certain denial of reality, a desire for an unnatural purity ... so that the beach can be the ideal desert, the empty stage, the naked shore, mirroring the unclothed body: a site henceforth exempt from nature and culture alike' (Urbain 2003: 138). The perfect beach, as it was dreamt up in Western imaginaries across the late nineteenth and twentieth centuries, is somewhere untouched by history, an almost literal *tabula rasa*, unmarked as well by apparently noxious littoral ecologies. Thus, the beach – not as a natural shorescape but as a cultural construction – is a Baudrillardian simulacrum, endlessly reproducible around the globe, a doppelgänger without a tangible original.[13]

In his seaside Gothic tale, 'Crooken Sands', Stoker luxuriates in the imagined freedoms of the beach, establishing the seaside as a realm of dramatic performativity and Gothic doubling in order to interrogate the integrity of the self and national identities. The significance of coastal environments to Stoker's writing will be evident to any reader of his fiction, given the iconic arrival by ship of Count Dracula into Whitby harbour in Stoker's most famous novel. More important than Whitby, however, to Stoker's work (and family holidays) is Cruden Bay, a Scottish village and seaside resort located between Aberdeen and Peterhead. Cruden Bay has a role to play in both *The Watter's Mou'* (1895) and *The Mystery of the Sea* (1902), and it is where Stoker is said to have drafted a great deal of *Dracula* (1897) (Shepherd 2018). It is given its most potent Gothic treatment, however, in 'Crooken Sands', where it is rechristened Crooken Bay. The story details the fairly dreadful summer holiday had by a London merchant, Arthur Fernlee Markam, and his family, who have taken a house in the bay. For the occasion, Markam, 'being essentially a cockney', considers it vital 'to provide an entire rig-out as a Highland chieftain', and he has had a tailoring firm in London supply him with a fabricated Highland costume in which he intends to strut about while in the coastal village (Stoker 2006: 129). Following endless ridicule from family and locals, and ominous warnings from a reputed local seer, Markam becomes haunted by his doppelgänger, who is encountered lingering on Crooken's beach. Eventually, the double is sucked into the depths of some quicksand and Markam, finally relenting, returns to his usual clothes. A letter at the end of the story suggests that Markam has mistaken for his double one of the London tailors, who was so enamoured of the Highland outfit that he too adopted it during his own vacation to Scotland.

The relationship between the Gothic, tourism, and performativity has received significant critical attention in recent years. In the context of nineteenth-century tourism to Cornwall, Joan Passey observes that 'Travel and tourism provided

---

[13] For further discussion of the Gothic beach see Packham (forthcoming).

opportunities for people to encounter the "Other" – new people, new places, new languages and new cultures' (Passey 2023: 95). Encounters between tourists and locals produce, for touristic consumption, elaborate or parodic versions of "authentic" cultural heritage, precipitating a 'rejection of and collusion with' the tourist industry while 'both exposing and eroding an ancient sense of Cornishness' (95, 94). Adopting a slightly different sense of performance, Emma McEvoy has highlighted how 'Gothic tourism' is self-reflexively performative, as theatrical productions – such as ghost walks – have become effective and *affective* staples of curated localised offerings to tourists (McEvoy 2016: 200–203). Yet another type of performance inflects seaside culture: the tourist as performer. For Hannah Freed-Thall, the modernists found at the beach the 'grounds on which to experiment with performances of embodiment and to devise a new grammar of sensation' (Freed-Thall 2023: 3). At the beach, one makes an exhibition of one's self; beaches provide 'a stage for the spectacle of leisure' and 'a showcase for the exhausted body' (163).

In Stoker's text, the Gothic heart of the holiday is indeed to be located in the tourist, who carries with them a ludic parody of the national cultures belonging to the nation in which they are temporarily resident. Markam's pantomimic performance of something vaguely approximating "Scottishness" is at least three or four removes from any plausible reality. Markam's tartanry operates within the wider nineteenth-century romanticisation and consumerist appropriation of Highland dress, especially tartan. This in turn participates in the deliberate, self-conscious forging of national identities underway in the nineteenth century *and* in a dislocation of culture, as tartan was co-opted to 'celebrat[e] British imperialism' (Brown 2010: 104). It is not surprising, then, that Markam's 'rig-out' is hardly Scottish, and obviously out of place on Scotland's east coast, far from the 'Highland chieftain[s]' he seeks to emulate. Markam takes inspiration from 'chromolithographs' and 'the music-hall stage' (Stoker 2006: 129), and though his London tailors trade under Scottish-sounding names – 'The Scotch All-wool Tartan clothing Mart', run by 'MacCallum More and Roderick MacDhu' – they speak with 'remarkable cockney accent[s]' (130–131). If there is any such thing as authenticity, it is in short supply indeed as Markam undertakes his sojourn to Crooken Bay. When he opts to make a spectacle of himself, parading in his outfit along the seashore, he is mockingly framed as a comic Gothic object by the bemused locals. Markam is told by one fisherman (speaking in Stoker's always overwrought dialect): 'Wully Beagrie thocht you was a ghaist, and Tom MacPhail swore ye was only like a goblin on a puddick-steel! "Na!" said I. "Yon's but the daft Englishman – the loony that has escapit frae the waxwarks"' (138). Is it a ghost, is it a goblin? No: it is an Englishman.

For all the fun that Markam's family, the local community, and Stoker himself, have with this seaside spectacle, there is a darker current eddying through the tale. This has its origins in Markam's encounter with his supposed doppelgänger and his fear that, as punishment for his vanity, he will be sucked into the beach's quicksand: for as the local seer warns him, 'Thy vanity is as the quicksand which swallows up all which comes within its spell.... See thyself!' (135). What Stoker's doppelgänger in fact shadows is not Markam alone, but the notion of touristic pastiche as a whole. Markam recognises the double as himself less via physiognomic similitude than by recognition of their shared costumery: the first glimpse of the doppelgänger on the beach is only of 'the bald back of the head and the Glengarry cap with the immense eagle's feather' (137). Later, Markam again encounters 'that fatal image of himself' (147). This time, the face is obscured in shadow, though he sees 'the same shaven cheeks as his own, and the small stubby moustache of a few weeks' growth'; while, by contrast, 'The light shone on the brilliant tartan', revealing the *outfit* as the most visible location of doubleness (147). The tourist is haunted by his own burlesque.

Moreover, it is really Markam, not this mysterious stranger, who is rhetorically associated with the figure of the doppelgänger: for these repeated seaside encounters 'lent aid to the conviction that he was in his own person an instance of the döppleganger' (145). The strange phrasing here renders Markam an uncanny simulacrum of himself, or the shadowy figure of the stereotypical tourist. If the touristic beach is always, to some degree, an encounter with a simulacrum, a space of bodily spectacle, (ideally) evacuated of history and culture, then Stoker taps into such notions for explicitly Gothic ends. The beach provides a stage on which the self is evacuated of itself, enabling a stark encounter with the illusion of selfhood and the murky realities of national identity. Markam never sees the face of his double: he stares at himself, but there is no self to be seen. He is recognisable only as an (inadequate) English imitation of a "Scottish" individual (who, as double, is not truly individuated).

The unsettled terrain of Stoker's beach offers another way to consider the politics of tourism as encoded in the story. Through Markam's encounters with the slough of seaside quicksand, Stoker posits the Gothic terror of touristic wandering. Markam becomes so obsessed with his double and the threat of his own inhumation in the quicksand that he continuously and unconsciously revisits this patch of shoreline. Waking one morning, he discovers 'a series of footsteps on the sands, which he at once recognised as his own'; following them, he sees that they become 'lost in the edge of the yielding quicksand' (143). Becoming as anxious as Crusoe, he repeatedly witnesses, 'oh, horror of horrors!', 'his own footprints dying into the abyss!' (145). Such recurrent encounters with his own inauspicious footfall resonates with what Lucie Armitt and Scott Brewster have identified as the 'peregrinatory Gothic', a mode in which tourists or travellers confront 'the shifting contours' of a region and its political and cultural histories; peregrinatory Gothic narratives 'place travellers on edge' literally and epistemically (Armitt and Brewster 2022: 95). The beachgoer's littoral 'performances of embodiment', to recall Freed-Thall, are transmuted, in Stoker's coastal Gothic, into a tendency towards obliteration and *dis*embodiment, as the self, evacuated of itself, makes somnambulistic footfall towards the landscape's most alluring yet threatening feature. Indeed, what is quicksand if not one of the landscape's most dramatically 'shifting contours'? It is a space, too, composed of far more *depth* than the ridiculous 'performances of embodiment' underway in its vicinity. When Markam's double and his own Highland costume are finally consumed by the quicksand, it is established as yet another of the coast's crypt-like archives, concealing in its depths the horrors of the beach holiday.

Stoker reserves much of his best prose for descriptions of this quicksand. He writes of how 'the liquid sand quivered and trembled and wrinkled and eddied as was its wont between its pauses of marble calm' (143) and of 'the wrinkly, crawling quicksand that seemed to writhe and yearn for something' (147). It is not just Stoker's prose that comes alive here: the quicksand is the text's ecoGothic centrepiece, animate and full of implied agency, its unsettlement echoed in the accumulation of adjectives that resist resolution. By way of conclusion to this section, I want briefly to dwell with the ecoGothic aspects of the seaside, as a means of setting up several ideas relevant to Section 3.

2.4 Seaweed, Samsung, and Aickman

In his cultural history of the beach, Urbain notes, as we have seen, that the seaside is a realm 'exempt from nature and culture alike'. 'Contemporary seaside vacationers', he observes, exhibit an especial 'phobia about seaweed'; 'its green and brown spots sully the model shore, dirty the dreamed-of beach' (Urbain 2003: 137). Such a notion would frame the typical modern beachgoer as engaging littoral ecologies in distinctly ecoGothic ways, specifically via an ecophobia – a 'contempt and fear ... for the agency of the natural environment' – that many, most notably Simon C. Estok, have suggested is foundational to ecoGothic narratives (Estok 2009: 207). A telling example of the persistence of this ecophobic relationship with essential marine plant-life can be found in a recent advertisement for a mobile phone produced by Samsung (Figure 2). The short commercial celebrates the phone's 'Photo Assist' function by showing AI technology magically abjecting seaweed from a couple's beach holiday photograph;

Figure 2 'See you seaweed!' (© Samsung Singapore 2024).

this is accompanied with the tagline 'From seaweed mess to beach bliss' (Samsung Singapore 2024).

While many in the nineteenth century would see tangible encounters with seaweed in much more positive terms – evidenced, for instance, by the widespread enthusiasm for kelp collecting – Gothic narratives from this period still find room to imagine the disquieting dimensions of algal entanglements. The *Blackwood's* tale 'Narrative of a Fatal Event' (1818) is a case in point.[14] The narrator recounts a six-week holiday he and a friend named Campbell had taken after completing their university studies. During a boating excursion into the Sound of Jura, Campbell falls overboard and is drowned: 'the boiling of the water, caused by his descending body, prevented a distinct view, but on looking down, I thought I saw three or four corpses, struggling with each other' (Anon. 1818: 632). As the waters settle, Campbell's eerie vitality haunts the narrator, who is granted a transgressive glimpse into the ordinarily obscure depths of the littoral world – a glimpse that neither Gaskell's tale nor Riddell's permits. Campbell appears

> to be yet alive, for he sat upright, and grasped with one hand the stem of a large tangle; the broad frond of which waved sometimes over him as it was moved by the tide, while he moved convulsively his other arm and one of his legs . . . . He then fell slowly on his back, and lay calm, and still, among the sea weed. (633)

Several questions concerning (eco)Gothic agencies inflect this sequence. Are the waters haunted by living corpses, or is this an illusion brought about by the turbid waters? Is Campbell himself still alive at the bottom of the Sound, or does the movement of the tide and the swaying of the seaweed impart the illusion of life? Most suggestive of all, perhaps, is the possibility that the several corpses perceived in the water are in fact swirling fronds of weed, indicative of a failure to differentiate between nonhuman and human after immersion in the littoral's aquatic depths.

A coastal encounter with noxious algae and the living dead is also the primary concern of Robert Aickman's 'Ringing the Changes' (1955). The story follows the ill-fated honeymoon of some newlyweds, Gerald and Phrynne, who have travelled for their holiday to a coastal village named Holihaven in East Anglia; they happen to arrive on the day the dead crawl out of earth and sea in order to frolic wildly with the local villagers. In this tale, the living dead become nauseatingly indistinguishable from the seaweed that litters Holihaven's uncomfortably expansive beach. When the newlyweds try to take a stroll down to the sea, they find they cannot: the sea has ebbed so far as to make it

---

[14] Authorship is usually attributed to Walter Scott or William Laidlaw.

unreachable and 'the smell of dense rotting weed' pervades the coast (Aickman 2014: 47–48). Armitt and Brewster offer a suggestively ecoGothic reading of Aickman's tale, noting that 'So extreme is the ebb tide in Holihaven, and so extreme the surge that follows, that Aickman might even be said to be writing a story about a ghostly tsunami' (Armitt and Brewster 2022: 51). It is a tale of littoral inundation, of becoming grotesquely, inescapably, saturated by the rank abjected matter that exists in and just off the nation's shorelines. As a piece of seaside Gothic, the uncanny affect of Aickman's tale is to be located both in the unwelcome encounter with a seaweed that seems to have marked every part of the coastal village, and in the encounter with a shoreline that provides simply *too much* beach.

The couple walk further and further across 'the desolate unattractive beach' (Aickman 2014: 49), inadvertently stepping in indiscernible foetid and muculent matter as they go. The tale reveals, and moves beyond, the utmost limit for experiencing littoral pleasure. The newlyweds fail to take a romantic stroll along the edge of the sea; instead, they find themselves walking beyond where the tideline *ought* to be, travelling across slippery ground that is usually seabed. This is not an encounter with the beautiful, but with a grotesque, Gothic sublime. Indeed, littoral matter is affectively overwhelming, transgressing its socially prescribed limits. The couple's hotel is located in 'Wrack Street' (41), an early sign of seaweed's centrality and abundance. When the dead later begin appearing in the town, our first glimpse is of 'something dark and shapeless' hurrying down the road (69). In their necrophilic rapture, the villagers are seen 'ecstatic and waving their arms above their heads' (73). And when the living and dead revellers burst into the hotel, the newlyweds are struck by 'the smell they had encountered on the beach . . ., no longer merely offensive, but obscene, unspeakable' (76).

From the perspective of Aickman's metropolitan outsiders, the human and vegetal dwellers on the shore are uncannily indistinguishable from one another. Recalling the littoral terror of 'Narrative of a Fatal Event', 'the dark and shapeless' corpses and the frond-like 'waving' arms of the villagers suggest a profound affinity and merging with the littoral environment. This thanatic coastal revelry has an overpowering impact on the outsiders' minds and senses of self: where Gerald's mind is battered into insensibility, Phyrnne is alluringly transformed by the celebrations. It is finally important to note that for the inhabitants of Holihaven this event is not wholly horrific, but an 'ecstatic' moment of Gothic communion with the dead *and*, more significantly for our current purposes, the supposedly abject matter of the shoreline. 'Ringing the Changes' suggests one way of "shoring up" identity at the shoreline is to embrace unsettlement, to let one be euphorically engulfed by that which the sea and littoral ground might give up, to embrace ebb and inundation. Confrontations with (eco)Gothic bodies travelling in and over water and onto the coast shape several of the texts under discussion in the next section, which turns to consider the important role of war in coastal Gothic narratives.

3 War and the Coastal Gothic

In its earliest years, the Gothic was engaged with the terrors of the French Revolution and the prospect of violence and war spilling onto British shores. Indeed, eighteenth-century Gothic literature capitalises on the fraught contest between two distinct spheres of experience: the castle – symbolic of patriarchal tyranny and military might – and a coast that troubles the legitimacy and longevity of the castle and those who inhabit it. This is a narrative trajectory we see in such foundational narratives as Horace Walpole's *The Castle of Otranto* (1764) and Ann Radcliffe's *A Sicilian Romance*. In both, labyrinthine caverns connected to the sea coast enable the return of the disinherited and the toppling of the castle's regime. In this section, I am interested in the abiding interest demonstrated by the coastal Gothic in narratives of war and invasion, and in the role of the coast as a site to mediate and meditate on international conflict. Where the previous section of this Element foregrounded coastal Gothic encounters between visitors and locals from within the British and Irish isles, this section examines the coastline as a preeminent site to reflect on questions of violence coming ashore from *beyond* the archipelago – though, as we will see, internecine terrors will continue to play an important role. This section structures its argument around several writers, including Rudyard Kipling, Sydney Owenson, Arthur Machen, and M. R. James, and it concludes with a reading of Adrian Ross' *The Hole of the Pit* (1914), a surprisingly neglected coastal Gothic novella set during the British Civil Wars (1642–1651) and published within the first few months of the First World War (1914–1918).

Given its archipelagic nature, it is hardly surprising that British rhetoric surrounding war and invasion has historically made much of the nation's coastline, as a barrier for defence *and* as a fragile and expansive point of entry. If, after the 1707 Act of Union, the British 'came to define themselves as a single people not because of any political or cultural consensus at home, but rather in reaction to the Other beyond their shores' (Colley 2003: 6), those 'shores' function as a vital marker of national identity: it is difficult to think of a more iconic example than the abundance of associations heaped upon the white cliffs of Dover (discussed in Section 4). Later in the eighteenth century, the anticipation of the spread of French Revolutionary violence and, relatedly, the prospect of war with France brought Britain's shores to the forefront of political debate.

In his 'Thoughts on the Impending Invasion of England' (1794), for instance, the abolitionist and Revolutionary sympathiser William Fox writes, with typical sarcasm,

> Fearful of hurting the high-toned feelings of the *True born Englishman*, we tremble to suppose it possible for the French to pass the twenty mile ditch which separates us; ... we will not even ask whether, in detached portions they may not take unknown tracts through the boundless ocean, and center upon our coasts; nor will we suggest a surmise, whether *Thuriot's* landing a thousand men and taking *Carrickfergus*, at a time when the French Navy was almost annihilated, be not something like a proof of its being possible. (Fox 1794: 12–13)

The seas surrounding Britain and Ireland, Fox implies, offer a fairly illusory bulwark against foreign incursion – more 'ditch' than ocean – as evidenced by the 1760 landing in Carrickfergus of French forces during the Seven Years War. 'Fears of French invasion seemed to be confirmed', writes Angela Wright, drawing on E. P. Thompson, 'in the February of 1797 when "the French actually made a small landing near Fishguard, on the Pembrokeshire coast"' (Wright 2013: 71). Edmund Burke gives a more overtly Gothic inflection to the matter of Revolutionary violence when he reads, in figurative terms, such violence as oceanic and peace as littoral. 'Were all these dreadful things necessary?' he asks in *Reflections on the Revolution in France* (1790): 'were they the inevitable results of the desperate struggle of determined patriots, compelled to wade through blood and tumult, to the quiet shore of a tranquil and prosperous liberty?' (the answer for Burke is a resounding 'No!' (Burke 1993: 39)).

3.1 Kipling and Owenson: Imperial Invasions

The Gothic thus came of age in an era when British and Irish shorelines were literal and – perhaps more significantly – powerfully symbolic sites of war and invasion anxiety. British national identity (especially as English nationalism) has continued to make use of the combined power of wartime episodes and the littoral: since the mid twentieth century, such rhetoric has turned most obviously on the Second World War (1939–1945). This conflict, as John Brannigan notes, 'had evidently heightened this sense of England as an island, that geographical misnomer so biased towards the view from the Sussex Downs'; Brannigan cites Winston Churchill's famous deployment of terms like 'this Island' and 'our Island', especially in the wake of the Dunkirk evacuations, to emphasise (not always accurately) a vision of the nation isolated, insular, standing alone

(Brannigan 2015: 222). In the late nineteenth and early twentieth centuries, too, the expansive scale of British, and European, colonialism was shadowed by anxieties about invasion: Ailise Bulfin has shown how 'in the fraught period between 1890 and 1914 paranoia about imminent war and invasion was again mounting' (Bulfin 2018: 10). Moreover, 'European rivalry over colonial possession engendered fears, not unfounded, of global war on a hitherto unseen scale, and the consequent occupation of Britain' (9). The Gothic, as Bulfin argues, responded with alacrity to such fears. The coastal Gothic has an important part to play in such imperial imaginaries.

We see this, for instance, in Rudyard Kipling's 'The Song of the Dead', a poem included in Kipling's strange series of interconnected poems, *A Song of the English* (1893). Even as 'The Song of the Dead' extols the reach of the British Empire and honours the memory of those who died in the name of continued imperial expansion, the poem registers a horrific vision of littoral zones around the globe. The oceans are so saturated by dead Englishmen that beaches worldwide are likely to be inundated with their corpses (see Figure 3 for W. Heath Robinson's illustration of these lines):

Figure 3 'But drops our dead on the sand'. Illustration by W. Heath Robinson (Kipling 1909: np). Retrieved from the Library of Congress: www.loc.gov/item/09030319/.

> We have fed our sea for a thousand years
>   And she calls us, still unfed,
> Though there's never a wave of all her waves
>   But marks our English dead:
> ...
> There's never an ebb goes seaward now
>   But drops our dead on the sand –
> But slinks our dead on the sands forlore,
>   From the Ducies to the Swin.
>
> (Kipling 1909: np)

From the South Pacific (Ducie Island is an atoll in the Pitcairn Islands) to English coastal waters (the Swin is part of the Thames Estuary), the beach is an English graveyard. Kipling's vision has no room for those subjected to English colonial violence; yet the poem also offers a fairly ghoulish account of the imperialism it is supposedly celebrating. England's colonial agents who make landfall on foreign shores are not living subjects but the dead, their agency dissipated, tossed about the globe by the unsettled motion of the oceans. England's colonial identity is forged, here, on its own self-extermination.

A richly sustained development of the relationship between the colonist, colonised, and coastal territory can also be found in Sydney Owenson's *The Wild Irish Girl* (1806): written in the wake of the 1800 Act for the Union of Great Britain and Ireland, the novel articulates a version of Irish national and cultural history entirely distinct from, and of far greater pedigree than, England and forms of Irish identity contingent on British presences in the Irish archipelago. (Owenson, however, struggles to imagine an Irish future that doesn't remain beholden to Britain.) Set in the late eighteenth century (prior to, but anticipating, the Act of Union), *The Wild Irish Girl* tells the story of Horatio M–, the exiled son of an English earl, sent to live on the earl's Irish estate in northwest Connacht, which 'fell into [the] family in the civil wars of Cromwell' (Owenson 2016: 41). Horatio becomes besotted with an Irish princess, Glorvina, whose ancestral lands, we learn, are those acquired by Horatio's forebears: while he woos Glorvina, Horatio keeps his real identity hidden from the princess and her father, the dispossessed and sickly Prince of Inismore. In a convoluted conclusion, identities are revealed, longstanding grudges are overcome, and Horatio and Glorvina are set to marry.[15] Coastal dwelling is central to the political topography mapped by *The Wild Irish Girl*.

Of his former estate, the Irish Prince retains only a small portion of land and an 'old ruined castle', whose rooms 'it had been said were haunted' (38), and in which

---

[15] The novel's marriage plot offers 'the now infamous "Glorvina solution" to the political divisions' of Britain and Ireland (Killeen 2014: 96).

he lives with his daughter, their Catholic priest, and a few retainers. The ruined castle is evocatively cut off physically from Ireland's mainland, too: it sits on a peninsula, and Horatio observes that a 'little isthmus … had been cut away, and a curious danger-threatening bridge was rudely thrown across the intervening gulf' (43). The Irish nobility are cast adrift from their ancestral homeland. Despite frequent reflections on the Gothic qualities of the castle, it is really the English colonists who function as the Gothic spectres haunting the Irish shore – and in quite self-conscious terms. Horatio refers to his 'wretched state of non-existence, this *articula mortis*' when describing his early experience of exile (34); later, he acknowledges his own '*memento mori* of a figure' (64); and in the novel's hectic climax, he is 'a figure, pale and ghastly' (231). Not unlike the portrayal given in Kipling, the English are the Gothic bodies on the shoreline. This is made all the more emphatic when we discover that Horatio's mostly absent father has *also* been trying to woo Glorvina – and in almost exactly the same manner as Horatio – in order to right the injustices wrought by colonial warfare. The English aristocrats are caught in a vaguely incestuous and uncanny cycle, each the other's doppelgänger, drifting in disguise along the Irish coast, occupying colonised ground and seeking to insinuate themselves, via Glorvina, into an indigenous and culturally valuable Irish lineage.

The coast of *The Wild Irish Girl* is also the site of national fortitude and protection. During one conversation, the Prince tells Horatio of the Irish soldiers 'called *Fynne Erin*, appointed to keep the sea coast, fearing foreign invasion, or foreign princes to enter the realm' (105). In his littoral castle, the Prince suggestively participates in this work: an idea heavily implied when, later in this same conversation, the English and Irish men begin 'battling about the country of Ossian' (111) – a verbal sparring echoing the martial acts of the Fynne Erin. Yet, of course, on the novel's terms, the Fynne Erin have failed: the coast has been breached, foreign nobility occupy Irish territory, and the Prince, in the sublime wreckage of his castle, is only a frail and ruinous version of the coast's historical guardians. The coast is the point at which Irish history and sovereignty have become frozen, caught at a moment of rupture.

Littoral Connacht is a Gothic (and reputedly haunted) archive and the Inismores have undergone something akin to a cultural shipwreck. At the heart of the castle is a room that 'serves as an armory, a museum, a cabinet of national antiquities, and national curiosities. In short, it is the receptacle of all those precious relics, which the Prince has been able to rescue from the wreck of his family splendour' (99). Cut off from the mainland, the castle performs the work of cultural preservation, but it is also, subject to the touristic gaze of the colonist, a cabinet of curiosities. Moreover, this littoral archive is imperilled by coastal erosion, as the stormy Atlantic will soon enough 'leave scarce a wreck to tell the traveller the mournful tale of fallen greatness' (61). Wreckage portends further – total – wreckage. For if the coast is a privileged site of Irish cultural identity and zone of preservation,[16] it is also an especially vulnerable environment for such work, threatened by elemental disintegration and by the Gothicised English invaders, whose spectral figurations – a Gothic iteration of Ireland's absentee landlords – are no barrier to continued possession of Irish territory. And if Owenson ultimately suggests that union with Britain is the only way to bring Irish cultural heritage back from the crumbling edgeland of history, this is no guarantee against future inhumation: a promised wedding between Horatio and Glorvina will see 'the distinctions of English and Irish, of protestant and catholic, for ever *buried*' (241: emphasis added).

3.2 Machen, War, and the Weird Coast

Owenson thinks about English colonisation within the margins of the British-Irish archipelago, and Kipling looks beyond these shores in order to imagine imperialism's global despoilation of the littoral. What is the effect, however, when an invasive presence brings war onto British shores, thus realising the political anxieties that have accompanied the Gothic since its emergence? One answer is given in the weird writing of Arthur Machen, particularly in those tales in which Machen reflects on the ways in which the First World War has left the world – and specifically the Welsh coast – profoundly unhinged. Images of deluge appear across Machen's best-known works about the Great War. The opening of 'The Bowmen' (1914) describes how 'three hundred thousand men in arms with all their artillery swelled like a flood against the little English company', while the longer narrative of wartime coastal violence, *The Terror* (1916), tells of how 'the German host swelled like a flood over the French fields' and how 'we felt the thrill of exultation when the good news came that the awful tide had been turned back' (Machen 2011: 223, 272). The specific prospect of war encroaching on British shores is given vivid treatment in the short sketch and allegory of wartime horror, 'Out of the Earth' (1915).

Machen's sketch is set in Castell Coch, 'a little bay bastioned by dunes and red sandstone cliffs, rich with greenery . . .; there is the ruined Norman Castle, the ancient church and the scattered village' (267).[17] This area of the Welsh coast has become popular since the onset of the Great War because, the narrator explains, fears of air-raids on Britain's east coast have driven holidaymakers

---

[16] Owenson's view here chimes with a longer literary tradition, identified by Nicholas Allen, 'in which Ireland has been imagined historically from the coastal margins and the near offshore' (Allen 2021: 10).

[17] While there is a real Castell Coch in Wales, it is located north of Cardiff and does not sit on the coast. *The Terror* also features Machen's coastal Castell Coch, where we learn that it sits on the country's south-west coast.

'westward for the first time' (266). The story details the episodes of intense violence, especially against children, that are breaking out along this stretch of shore. A companion of the narrator's named Morgan reveals, after encountering the agents of this violence first-hand, that it is being enacted by 'a swarm of noisome children, horrible little stunted creatures with old men's faces, with bloated faces, with little sunken eyes, with leering eyes' (270). Morgan avers that 'These little people of the earth rise up and rejoice in these times of ours. For they are glad . . . when they know that men follow their ways' (271). Their language, we are told, is especially loathsome, as they utter

> horrible raucous cries – and the cries of children, too, but children of the lowest type. . . . 'They were to the ear what slime is to the touch,' and then the words: every foulness, every filthy abomination of speech; blasphemies that struck like blows at the sky, that sank down into the pure, shining depths, defiling them! (270)

These remarks achieve two things. They suggest, first, a viable reading of the tale within a regionalist Gothic framework: the English trippers to the Welsh coast in search of peace find themselves, or so they believe, face-to-face with 'a pack of young Welsh savages' (268). Instead of unifying the nation in a time of national crisis, the Great War has disrupted routines and necessitated eerie encounters with the metropolitan centre's peripheral Others.

The remarks also tie Machen's wartime horror tale into his 'little people' mythology, though it uses them in ways quite different to his earlier weird fiction. This mythology, Emily Alder explains, 'constructs an enweirded history' – a more-than-human history that might also be an alternative national history – 'that, if it were to be true, explodes the consensus reality of what history is (or was) and demands acceptance of an alternative or co-existing, even conflicting, history existing in parallel' (Alder 2020: 60). Their presence across numerous of Machen's tales is in keeping with his insistence 'that a wondrous reality lies beyond the everyday, but the capacity of the modern world's state of knowledge to understand it is severely limited, especially by its narrow materialism' (55). One gains access to this 'enweirded history' and 'wondrous reality' partly by chance, partly by retaining a childlike worldview, and by the passing-down of local occult folk practices and knowledge, as we see for example in 'The Shining Pyramid' (1895) and 'The White People' (1904). Machen usually locates his little people deep in entangled woodlands and amid inland hills and hollows. In 'Out of the Earth', however, the Great War appears to have drawn them to the coast – displaced from their usual haunts in the manner of the English tourists. In this way, the Great War is itself an 'enweirding' ecoGothic force, rendering perilously thin the veil that normally separates our world from the other worlds that reside within or behind it.

As allegorical figures of this war, the little people of 'Out of the Earth' manifest a devastating violence that has made landfall on British shores: their voices, for instance, are incomprehensible, literalising the trope of war's unspeakability, and incendiary, striking 'like blows at the sky' and 'defiling' the coastal waters into which they sink (the strange, Poe-like observation that their voices 'were to the ear what slime is to the touch' will chime with the upcoming discussion of Adrian Ross). Like *The Terror*, this story suggests that a physical invasion is not necessary in order to plunge the nation into chaos and violence: the war has shifted the contours of the world such that its very atmosphere has become charged with existential terrors, and the infernal realm, usually hidden, has breached the material world in broad daylight. Yet, perhaps, what the Great War and the little people who delight in it really achieve is not an unmaking of our peaceable island and its tranquil shores. Instead, the coastal terror the war forebodes, and which these creatures enact, alerts us to the long and deep history of war and conflict to even seemingly remote shorelines of the archipelago. They remind us that, before it becomes a picturesque holiday destination, the coast is foremost a site of military activity and integral to displays of national power: the coastal topography and its weird inhabitants demonstrate that war is intrinsic to national identity and integrity and not (or not only) an existential threat to it. Machen's little people disclose a 'conflicting' history, recalling Alder's words, *and* a history of conflict, history *as* conflict.

As we have seen, the tale emphasises that Castell Coch is named for 'the ruined Norman Castle' on the cliffs – a typical Gothic ruin that contributes to the 'peace and quiet and great beauty' of the region (Machen 2011: 267), which also recalls what might be termed Britain's (certainly England's) *ur*-invasion narrative, the Norman Conquest of 1066. Morgan's brush with the little people also occurs on suggestively martial ground, in the ruins of an ancient fort on a headland known as 'the Old Camp', where are 'solemn, mighty walls, turf-grown; circumvallations rounded and smooth with the passing of many thousand years' (270). The weird war being waged by the little people is not exactly out of kilter with this setting. Indeed, the great antiquity of these ruins – 'rounded and smooth with the passing of many thousand years', significantly predating the Norman castle – echoes the agedness associated with the little people. This fortification has long since sunk into the earth, becoming 'turf-grown', a Gothicised piece of architecture sitting somewhere between the artificial and the natural. Yet it, too, like the little people, continues to erupt 'Out of the Earth'. Thus, Machen's story does not merely unearth the more-than-human horrors that shadow (and thrive on) our own horrific human histories.

But it also unearths the human presence within that more-than-human world, bringing to mind the fact that even the soft undulating contours of the coastal landscape of this remote headland tell a story of enduring human conflict.

The unearthing of signifiers of international and (un)holy warfare is central, too, to the celebrated coastal Gothic stories of M. R. James. The occult objects buried in and unwisely excavated from the coastal ground in both 'Oh, Whistle, and I'll Come to You, My Lad' and 'A Warning to the Curious' explicitly frame the Suffolk coast, which James knew well, as a martial realm, a zone of confrontation between different powers, worldly and otherwise.

3.3 Beaches and Breaches in James

The presence of war in 'A Warning to the Curious' is already well documented. The story concerns the legend of three holy crowns that have been 'buried in different places near the coast to keep off the Danes or the French or the Germans' (James 2011: 346) – a contingent of foreign powers that maps a changing sense of England's foreign Other (to recall Colley's terminology). One of these crowns, we learn, 'was dug up a long time ago, and another has disappeared by the encroaching of the sea', so that there is only one 'left doing its work, keeping off invaders' (346). The final crown, it transpires, has been discovered on the coast at Seaburgh (a fictional version of Aldeburgh) by a man named Paxton, who finds himself pursued by a supernatural presence after he unearths it, thus potentially compromising the nation's mystically safeguarded borders: this presence is likely a (ghostly) member of the Ager family, who had been tasked with defending the buried crown, as they had during the earlier 'war of 1870' and 'the South African War' (347). With several companions, Paxton attempts to reinter the object, but it is no use: *something* continues to haunt him and he is found, by the end of the tale, with his face violently smashed to pieces on the shoreline.

The tale, Patrick J. Murphy argues, can be read as a moving effort by James to make some sense of the First World War, offering 'a bereaved mentor's rumination on war and its memory, both collective and personal, commemorative and corrosive' (Murphy 2017: 173). 'A Warning to the Curious' makes especially evocative use of a coastal war memorial located in Aldeburgh, the text of which was composed by James himself, as part of his work in providing memorials to the war dead (168–169). As Andrew Smith has recently noted, James' engagement with the Great War might be seen to pull in two different directions. One version of James is 'the man of public office who wants the war dead to be remembered with affection, while the other is the writer of ghost stories in which images of the solider-dead are not recalled in such a benign, or sanitised, way', as Paxton's violent death, especially his facial wounding, 'represents the type of aggression associated with British nationalism and its view of the Germans' (Smith 2022: 167). The coastal perspective of 'A Warning to the Curious' is bifurcated in perhaps another way, too: like Machen, James seeks to confront one war by looking (or looking away) towards other conflicts. If 'A Warning to the Curious' addresses anxieties about national invasion in the context of the Great War, it contextualises these anxieties within a much longer historical vision of an England repeatedly (*always*) threatened by foreign powers, for, as one knowledgeable local in the tale puts it, 'if it hadn't have been for one of them 'oly crowns bein' there still, them Germans would a landed here time and again, they would' (James 2011: 345). In the wake of the Great War, James takes us to the coast to look across the North Sea towards Europe and appreciate the precarity of our national defences.

While 'A Warning to the Curious' offers James' most direct engagement with questions of the coast, war, and invasion, I want now to turn back to his earlier piece of coastal Gothic, 'Oh, Whistle, and I'll Come to You, My Lad', in order to speculate on this tale's involvement with similar concerns. This text offers a rather more scattered perspective on international warfare than his later tale of the Great War, though the insistence by which 'Oh, Whistle' turns to images of conflict and historical and spiritual war suggests that James had long found the coast a rich location to dwell on the themes that find their final expression in 'A Warning to the Curious'. Indeed, though James is rarely read as an author concerned with British imperialism, 'Oh, Whistle' might nonetheless be situated, albeit obliquely, within a context that shows Britain as involved in a series of conflicts that exist far beyond, but nonetheless have an impact on, its shores. The text is published, after all, in the midpoint of the period identified by Bulfin as a time rife with invasion narratives and anxieties about the fate of Europe's various empires (1890–1914).

'Oh, Whistle' details the terrors that beset a Cambridge academic, Professor Parkins, during an out-of-season jaunt to the seaside town of Burnstow (a fictional Felixstowe), after he excavates and blows on a whistle found buried in some ruins near the beach. Like 'A Warning to the Curious', the tale's seaside excursions take place within view of buildings with explicitly martial designations, most notably 'the squat martello tower' (James 2011: 81) – part of a series of towers erected along the coasts of Britain and Ireland in the early nineteenth century, designed to protect against potential invasion by Napoleon Bonaparte. More significant, however, is 'the ruined Templars' church' (81), or preceptory, in whose crumbling foundations Parkins finds the haunted whistle, and which, like Machen's castell, has become 'grown over with turf' (79). The coastal ruin and the Gothic object it houses belong(ed), this tells us, to the Knights Templar, a religious military order founded in the early twelfth century, in the aftermath of the First Crusade (1096–1099) and the development of so-called 'Crusader States' in the Levant, in order to 'defend pilgrims in the Holy Land' (Phillips 2014: 68). Indeed, the Templars 'were a direct product of the crusades – not only because protection of the holy places was an avowed aim of the First Crusade, but also in as much as the notion of a knight dedicated to a religious purpose while remaining an active warrior was fully comprehensible after 1095' (Jotischky 2013: 80).

Thus when Parkins plucks the whistle from the soil of the English coast, he is making contact with an object that carries with it connotations of religious and international warfare and European colonisation of western Asian territories.[18] It is in this context that we might understand the effect of the blowing of the whistle on Parkins, which 'had a quality of infinite distance in it' and seems to Parkins like 'it must be audible for miles round', conjuring 'a vision of a wide, dark expanse at night' (James 2011: 83). The whistle evokes vast *distance*, dislocating Parkins, it seems, from his immediate littoral surroundings; the whistle suggestively gestures towards the elsewheres with which it is connected. The collapsing of England's shores with its more distant colonies is also hinted at during the tale's conclusion when Parkins' golfing companion, Colonel Wilson (another martial figure, 'an *ancien militaire*' (79), haunting the seaside during its unseasonable months) connects Parkins' night terrors with 'a not very dissimilar occurrence in India' (93): a brief glimpse of the nation's contemporary colonial activities. As if nudging us to see littoral space in distinctly *global* terms, we might also note that Parkins is staying at 'the Globe Inn' (79), which, due to coastal erosion, is getting closer and closer to the ocean that connects the British Empire with the nations it has colonised.

Several features of Burnstow portray the nation's shoreline less as a parochial and unsteady boundary-point of that nation, and rather emphasise that nation's global presence, a presence predicated on war and colonial endeavours. Parkins, too, is several times framed as a figure involved in forms of spiritual or religious conflict.[19] Direct references to the Book of Daniel and to Christian's encounter with Apollyon in *The Pilgrim's Progress* (1678/1684) stress Parkins' awareness that earlier episodes of religious warfare shadow his activities. While these allusions are briefly made, they nonetheless work to shore up the text's sense of the littoral world as a battleground and conflict zone, a realm where one's kingdom and one's self – and *soul* – may well be imperilled. But spiritual and

---

[18] On the complexity of reading the crusades as a 'colonial' venture (as modern readers would understand that term) see Jotischky (2013: 16–22).

[19] Relatedly, Murphy notes that James' text (somewhat bathetically) 'position[s] Parkins as a kind of knight errant in training (Murphy 2017: 43).

historical precedents are not the only way by which the integrity of the nation, and those who dwell within its shores, are imperilled in James' seaside Gothic stories. The shoreline itself is eroding away: the loss of the littoral environment that marks both 'Oh, Whistle' and 'A Warning to the Curious' suggests the futility of *any* efforts humans might make to fortify the nation against invasive forces.

'The sea has encroached tremendously' on Burnstow, Parkins is told near the start of 'Oh, Whistle' (76). This is especially pronounced near the academic's holiday lodgings, for 'Whatever may have been the original distance between the Globe Inn and the sea, not more than sixty yards now separated them' (79). When it comes to 'A Warning to the Curious', we have already seen that one crown has been lost to 'the encroaching of the sea' (words that uncannily double those from James' earlier tale), as it is speculated that it was held in 'a Saxon royal palace which is now under the sea' (346) – an allusion to Dunwich, once the capital of the Kingdom of East Anglia and now largely lost to the sea. Moreover, 'the old battery, close to the sea' that existed, though a ruin, at the time of the narrative's events has, at the time of the narrative's telling, more or less totally vanished: 'there are only a few blocks of concrete left now: the rest has all been washed away' (356).

Parkins' and Paxton's indiscretions look fairly tame against this backdrop of ongoing and large-scale littoral erosion. Given the alarming pace at which land is crumbling into the sea, the whistle and the crown were surely unlikely to remain buried for much longer, no matter how wide a berth human interlopers might give them. Indeed, it is 'precisely because of the unstable geological composition of that land', writes Lucie Armitt, that 'excavations into it are depicted as being dangerously easy' (Armitt 2016: 98). For Armitt, the supernatural terrors of James' tales partake of the territorial and elemental instabilities that characterise coastal East Anglia. It is not human invasion but oceanic inundation that poses the most tangible threat to the nation's littoral borderlands. In the littoral world, everything is tending towards a kind of vanishment or effacement, crumpling and crumbling.

The effect of this elemental violence is the erasure at the shore of identifying marks – from supernatural footprints to the coastal battery, to entire port-towns like Dunwich. The prospect of indistinguishability is central to the Gothic terror of 'Oh, Whistle'. The 'pale, fluttering draperies' of the spectral figure in Parkins' nightmare, which drifts like littoral matter lifted by the tides 'across the beach to the water-edge and back again' (James 2011: 85), has its echo in an earlier description of the beach's 'pale ribbon of sands' (81): the vengeful ghost from the Templar's preceptory converges with the littoral shorescape. More to the point, Parkins cannot tell one beach from another: the 'long stretch of shore' he sees in his night-vision, appears 'so like that of his afternoon's walk that, in the absence of any landmark, it could not be distinguished therefrom' (84). It is not totally clear whether we are meant to read these beaches as the *same* beach, or see the nightmare beach as a Gothic doppelgänger of the original beach, or – most horrifying of all, perhaps – understand that the beach has a tendency towards indecipherability. The shoreline, that is, becomes illegible, due to the disintegration of the land by and into the sea; *our* beach thus becomes difficult to distinguish from the Gothic beach, from its uncanny Other. In this way, the limits of the nation become perilously indistinct.

3.4 Ross, Civil Wars, and Slime

The meditations on national and individual fortitude in 'Oh, Whistle' and 'A Warning to the Curious' take place on littoral terrain characterised by fragmentation; the shorescape is swept by sea and mist, certainly, but the emphasis falls throughout on loose grains of sand and shingle, a terrain across which one might stumble and slip. By travelling north towards the Wash, we encounter a sea-soaked landscape, or land-marked seascape, whose predominating features in the coastal Gothic imagination are marsh, ooze, and – as *The Hole of the Pit* repeatedly stresses – *slime*. With precious little by way of firm footholds, this is a region by which one is enveloped and engulfed. And envelopment and engulfment is precisely what awaits the majority of the characters in Adrian Ross' idiosyncratic novel.

Dedicated to Ross' friend and colleague M. R. James, *Hole of the Pit* is set in the aftermath of the Battle of Naseby (1645), in the midst of the British Civil Wars. It concerns itself with a contingent of royalists led by the fictional Earl of Deeping, who, having fled Naseby, have taken refuge in the earl's ancestral home, Deeping Hold, a teetering fortification located 'in the sea-marshes at the mouth of the river Bere' (Ross 2010: 65). The castle is largely inaccessible except by boat, save at low tide when one might traverse a path 'winding, slippery, and beset with quicksands' (79). We follow Hubert Leyton, a cousin of the earl and notionally nonpartisan actor in the wars,[20] who has been sent to the castle as an emissary of peace on behalf of the residents of nearby Marsham, who find themselves subjected to the royalists' capricious violence; Leyton swiftly goes from emissary to captive. Events hurtle towards their end: namely, the fulfilment of a longstanding prophecy foretelling the doom of Deeping Hold. Even by Gothic standards, *Hole of the Pit* is over-stuffed with ominous

---

[20] As Imogen Peck has noted, Leyton's nonpartisan stance is both impossible to sustain in the midst of a civil war and relies fundamentally 'on a longstanding friendship with Cromwell, which, though it is personal rather than partisan, is the only thing that can protect him' (Peck 2024: 280).

forces of threat and unease. Alongside the parliamentarian troops marching inexorably towards the royalists, the novel features a malevolent Italian sorceress or necromancer, the briefly glimpsed ghost of a murdered noblewoman, and, pulsing in the waters of the Wash, seemingly sentient slime and/or a tentacled monstrosity, whose appearance, like Tennyson's kraken, heralds an apocalyptic reckoning for Deeping's unhappy earl.

While the Civil Wars, and the implications of a polity split against itself, are the most obvious concerns of Ross' novel, the text is first published in October 1914, not more than three months after the outbreak of the First World War. This timing inevitably means the novel cannot be offering sustained consideration of the Great War's impact on nations or individuals in the manner of 'A Warning to the Curious'. But *Hole of the Pit* is nonetheless marked by continuous reflections on European wars, notably 'the German wars', that is, the Thirty Years' War (1618–1648). In this section's final discussion, then, I offer some remarks on the novel's bringing together of its slime-filled littoral environment, the British Civil Wars, and the Great War.

As a novel of the Civil Wars, the implicit East Anglian setting of *Hole of the Pit* establishes the action within a region marked by widespread parliamentarian support (and the birthplace of Oliver Cromwell, derisively nicknamed "the Lord of the Fens"): small wonder that the royalist forces at the heart of the novel should feel besieged from all angles. The seventeenth-century setting of the novel also takes in the period in which a sustained programme of development, draining, and "reclamation" began across East Anglia's vast fenlands, pioneered by Dutch engineers such as Cornelius Vermuyden (Ash 2017). In fact and the literary imagination, the fens are a fluctuating topography, presenting a series of submergences and re-surfacings, of things going under and coming up again, of matter(s) being only ever temporarily repressed. Indeed, Lowell Duckert describes England's relationship with its fens in distinctly martial terms: 'early modern forays into the fens tell us about humanity's ongoing fight against the quagmire, a transhistorical assault that can never seem to reach a ceasefire' (Duckert 2017: 204). *Hole of the Pit* concerns, then, a nation at war with itself and, in the context of the fens, its own territory, as seethingly alive as the creature that dwells in the waters. This wetscape is as unsettled as the internecine conflict playing out across it: littoral geography reflects (even enacts) national history.

Hole of the Pit, in fact, frequently collapses the distinction between the threat posed by civil conflict and the monster lurking in littoral depths, a 'coiling streak of grey slime' encompassing the fortification in a way that anticipates the imminent besiegement by parliamentary forces (Ross 2010: 115). Indeed, as the parliamentarians never actually arrive, the Gothic monster *stands in* for this force and the royalists' vanquishment – a monstrous herald of the approaching republics. When Leyton considers murdering his cousin for the greater good, he argues, in distinctly providential terms, that whether the earl's killer is 'one of Cromwell's troopers, or a traitor of his own men, or a monster of the great deep, mattered little', for the agent would be 'but an instrument in God's hand' (142). The earl, too, intends to 'baulk Roundheads or monsters of my life' (162). And by the end of the story, when all threats are vanquished, Leyton has decided to 'say naught of the Thing that had dwelt in the Hole, nor of what of strange and monstrous had happened to our company' (187): events are to be explicable, then, only as part of the Civil Wars, into whose narrative the monster is silently subsumed as invisible but consequential actant. The monster must somehow be *forgotten* within a narrative of the Civil Wars in order to curate some semblance of closure to the wars' devastation.

The littoral topography of the novel – set in a castle built on a rocky islet in the midst of the Wash – also enables Ross to tell an expansively *international* story of the Civil Wars. The island provides a microcosmic vision of a nation turned upside down. Here, Leyton charts his changing perception of England, as he travels to Deeping Hold:

> the prospect, though fair enough on a morning of sunshine, was such as, thank God, a man could still see on many roads of our England, where even civil war had not roused up Croats or Pandours to burn and plunder foe and friend. But now came in the strangeness of that countryside . . ., I beheld a waste of grey sea-marsh, seamed and scarred . . . and I could note nothing clearly, save that on the very edge of the world, as it were, I caught the dazzle of the open sea. (70–71)

As Leyton travels towards the littoral conflict zone, the nation seems to dissolve before him, such that he is on 'the very edge of the world': the coast is dislocated from the nation, yet civil conflict has engulfed even this realm. In this edgeland, the Civil Wars are shown to be conducted via a diverse array of international players, 'For here you had not plain honest English wickedness alone, but the flower of the rascals of all nations' (83). Alongside the English, 'Croats', and 'Pandours' already mentioned, the war is conducted in *Hole of the Pit* via an Italian sorceress, a North African Moor, and Irish, German, Spanish, and Swedish troopers.

The earl's villainy, then, lies in part in his accommodation of foreign scoundrels, who come seeking possession of English soil; it is perhaps for this reason that Leyton's vision of England deliquesces as he reaches the nation's strange outer limits. These foreign agents also function as a means by which Ross can largely exonerate the English of the wars' most heinous crimes (after all, they exhibit only plain *honest* wickedness); foreigners instead are responsible for the conflict's worst excesses. Of particular significance in this respect are those who participated in 'the German wars', which is where the earl 'learnt his warfare' (67). In the seventeenth-century imagination, the Thirty Years' War provided a grim counterpart to the British conflict, an awful forewarning of the possibility of extended and savage bloodshed.[21] The novel's repeated invocations of 'the German wars' and the prospect of pan-European warfare also provides the opportunity to move from the seventeenth to the twentieth century, and consider the text's (anticipatory) relationship with the Great War. As Imogen Peck has shown, contemporary reviews of Ross' novel were curiously keen to emphasise that *Hole of the Pit* 'has nothing to do' with the war that had recently broken out in Europe. This seems, Peck observes, 'like an act of wilful misinterpretation' – or perhaps psychological distancing – since the novel articulates so clearly 'the anxieties of a nation teetering on the edge of war' (Peck 2024: 280). The text, as we have seen, obsesses over the intrusion into Britain of the soldiers of 'the German wars'. Further, the novel's distinctly ecoGothic preoccupation with an interstitial landscape, slime, and frustrated burial can be seen curiously to anticipate important aspects of the Great War's figuration in literature, which would develop over the coming years.

Ross' figuration of a littoral zone saturated by the rank, abject matter of slime returns us to an image of the coast we have previously encountered via Aickman's 'Ringing the Changes': here, too, slime, a grotesque interstitial ecoGothic agent, presents an existential threat to humans and their habitations. Leyton watches in horror as he sees 'slimy jelly seething through the shallow water' towards his love interest, Rosamund Fanshaw, before it then begins 'oozing seaward over the rocks', having ensnared her (Ross 2010: 158). To some degree, *Hole of the Pit* conforms to Susanne Wedlich's evocative claim that slime often 'embodies the blurred line between us and the Other': 'Our boundaries are fluid enough in reality. And they are marked in slime' (Wedlich 2022: 17–18). In notably Gothic terms, slime 'represents the crossing of the last barrier between life and death, when the body loses all definition during slimy decomposition'; slime signifies 'breakdown and a loss of order' (18). In Ross' novel, slime continuously makes its presence known, until eventually there is 'slime oozing through the cracks' of the castle (Ross 2010: 168), the human-built edifice subsumed by the region's pulsating wetscape. This Element has already suggested that the coast is a site of unburial, where the corpse becomes unnervingly *visible*. Slime does something that is arguably worse: the littoral slimeworld of *Hole of the Pit* evacuates the shroud and the grave of the human bodies they ought to keep and conceal – the corpse vanishes.

---

[21] On Britain and the Thirty Years' War see Roy (1978).

When one man is sadistically cast into the Wash to be consumed by the monster, his armour is recovered, 'smeared with the grey slime'; lifting the armour's visor, the executioners find 'the face was gone, and only empty blackness within' (109). Later, a burial party seeks to inter several corpses on a small mound of earth: as the task is completed, the mound

> crumbled away with a loud sucking sound, and where the hillock had been was a yeasty whirl of grey sand and water and slime . . ., and in the midst of it one of the corpses, with the shroud gone from it, and the dead hands turning as though in strife to escape . . . . Yet, as I gazed, the body was drawn down slowly into the water, the tendrils of slime seeming to tighten around it like cords[.] (117)

The eerie animacy of the dead body recalls that imparted by the seaweed discussed in Section 2. Moreover, the coast is a realm of death and desolation, whose many corpses become unlocatable, undergoing profound erasure in the environment's aquatic depths. Ross' portrayal of missing bodies and of an international war undertaken through, and against, an obliterative mass of slime provides several means by which his novel begins to dovetail with the literature of the Great War. For swamp and slime are key actants in what might be termed the Great War's ecoGothic imaginary. Over the course of the war, notes Rod Giblett, 'land was turned into artificial wetland'; even in death, Giblett shows via the poetry of Siegfried Sassoon, 'there was no escaping from slime and mud. The Dead lived on in slime' (Giblett 2009: 59). *Hole of the Pit* may only be a literary artefact of the Great War if we, like Emily Dickinson, tell its history but tell it slant. Nevertheless, this work of coastal ecoGothic turns its gaze towards European combatants and emphasises the overwhelmingly slimy nature of the battlefield, thereby providing a sign of things to come.

4 Migration and the Coastal Uncanny

John Lanchester's dystopian novel *The Wall* (2019) represents a logical extension of the coastal Gothic narratives of littoral fortification examined in the previous section. In Lanchester's novel, Britain's insularity and extensive coastal borders have been secured by the building of a wall 'ten thousand kilometres long, more or less', around the coastline (Lanchester 2019: 14). The littoral borders of states can be secured, it seems, only when there is no more coast to speak of: another island is described as 'beachless, like every coastline in the world', rising 'vertically out of the sea' (199). The wall has been necessitated by rising sea-levels following what the novel terms 'the Change', and while helping to secure the island's territorial integrity against the devastating effects of climate change, the wall's other – and, indeed, principal – purpose is to keep out what the novel refers to in no uncertain terms as 'the Others': migrants and climate refugees seeking the relative safety of extant habitable land. Armed guards patrol the wall, tasked with killing anyone who attempts to breach the structure.

With its overt interest in the contest between selves and Others, and, as the plot develops, the overlaps between these two subject positions, *The Wall* moves from dystopian towards recognisably Gothic territory. In his efforts to imagine things from the perspective of the Other, the novel's protagonist acknowledges that 'the Wall must look like a terrible thing from the sea, a flat malevolent line like a scar' (65) and that 'We must seem more like devils than human beings. Spirits, embodied essences, of pure malignity' (66). What transformations must the self, the citizen (or, here, defender) of the nation, undergo in order to secure that selfhood and the littoral edgelands that mark its limits against the Other who, so it is feared, troubles the foundations of both self and state? Indeed, *The Wall* represents perhaps the purest form of coastal Gothic invasion narrative in its portrait of Britain as an island that exists in a perpetual state of fending off potential "invaders": in this world, one is either defender or invader.

Lanchester's novel is clearly responding to contemporary political discourse around migration, especially the rhetoric associated with the 'Brexit' referendum of 2016: *The Wall*, Christine Berberich has noted, 'takes the fear of incomers to the next level and presents an alternative reality where the country refuses to engage with migration altogether' (Berberich 2023: 40). Dover's white cliffs – to which I return below – played an especially valuable role for those campaigning for Britain to leave the European Union during the Brexit referendum: the cliffs, as Roger Luckhurst puts it in his discussion of Brexit's Gothic discourse, were the 'emblematic wall ... that holds back the pollutants of Europe or relentless invasion by global migrants' (Luckhurst 2023: 327). Indeed, the virulent rhetoric around British immigration in the second decade of the twenty-first century – designed to foster what former UK Prime Minister Theresa May infamously designated a 'hostile environment' for migrants – often turns to the coastline as a site where migration becomes potently visible, literally and symbolically. Another former Prime Minister, David Cameron, spoke in 2015 of the 'swarms' of migrants crossing the Mediterranean en route to Britain (BBC News 2015), while between 2023 and 2024 yet another former Prime Minister, Rishi Sunak, targeted the small and often extremely unsafe vessels carrying migrants across the English Channel via his frantically reiterated mantra that the Conservative Party will 'stop the boats' (Sunak 2024). And in May 2025 Sunak's successor in Downing Street, the Labour Party's Keir

Starmer, proposed that unregulated immigration would transform Britain into an 'island of strangers' – a term deeply entangled with the language of coastal Gothic as discussed across this Element (Starmer 2025).

Hostile environments and Gothic rhetoric surrounding migration are not, of course, recent phenomena. There has long been a conspicuous intersection between Gothic fiction and a Gothicised rhetoric pertaining to migration, with both latching onto the coast as a powerful environment in the articulation of state-endorsed attitudes (often negative and hostile) towards those migrants or refugees who land on its shores. Lanchester's *The Wall* sits within a lineage of coastal Gothic invasion narratives traceable back to the *fin de siècle* when, as Ailise Bulfin has shown, anxieties about invasion into Britain were rife. It goes back further, too, to the late eighteenth century and accounts of French emigration to Britain during the Revolution and its terrors. For the remainder of this section, I turn back to this longer history of coastal Gothic migration narratives, focusing in particular on Frances Burney's *The Wanderer*, Joseph Conrad's 'Amy Foster' (1901), and Helen Oyeyemi's *White is For Witching* (2009). In their accounts of migrants making landfall on England's south coast, a Gothic perspective is frequently discernible in those British characters who seek to comprehend, to render *legible*, the figure of the migrant. That is, while texts such as Burney's or Conrad's might not be conventionally or wholly Gothic, the Gothic nevertheless has an important function in their portrait of coastal encounters, rooted particularly in the affective power of the uncanny.

4.1 Burney, Legibility, and the Uncanny Émigrée

The greatest influx of Revolutionary émigrés and exiles from France occurred during the Reign of Terror, following the September massacres in 1792. 'By the end of September', writes Kirsty Carpenter, 'hundreds of refugees were arriving daily along a stretch of coast from Dover to Southampton': 'it was the nearest that the eighteenth century came to producing "boat people"' (Carpenter 1999: 30, 29). Fears that some of these arrivals on British shores were not simply exiles from France but were spies and agents of the Revolution, prompted the passing in Britain of the Aliens Act in January 1793: the act 'forc[ed] all foreigners to register at customs' and functioned as 'the first official immigration registration system' (Reboul 2017: 43, 64). If, as Juliette Reboul has suggested, the émigrés 'had metaphorically become aliens to the revolutionary project' by leaving France, so were they explicitly alien-ated once more via the Aliens Act (5). Moreover, though the coast is the obvious point of *arrival* for French migrants, it was not a space in which British authorities wished foreigners to *dwell*: from February 1793, 'aliens' were expected to reside at least ten miles from the coast and the six Royal Dockyards (68). As a readily accessible part of the state, the coast is a point of refuge *and* unsettlement – a site in which settlement is explicitly a cause for some concern, in light of ongoing fears about French invasion. It is a realm that might readily harbour secrets. Such anxieties speak to the issue of the legibility of the figure of the emigrant: who exactly is the émigré(e)? This is the question that motivates much of Frances Burney's final novel, *The Wanderer*.

Burney's novel unfolds for the most part along England's southern coast – between Dover and Brighton – with brief forays towards London and Stonehenge and an opening sequence involving the French coast and English Channel. The plot concerns a young woman who, after being smuggled out of France and into Dover, attempts to establish herself within English society while hiding the truth of her identity from those around her. We gradually learn that the woman, Juliet Granville, is the (secret) daughter of an English earl, brought up by guardians in France, and returning to England to escape the Revolution and a forced marriage to a French commissary (who had sought thereby to acquire Juliet's inheritance). While the novel ends happily – Juliet's identity is restored, her French husband is deported and executed, and she marries the man she met on her Channel crossing – an array of Gothicisims inflect much of *The Wanderer*'s frantic plotting: family secrets, misidentifications, obfuscating silences, lost documentation and objects, and the ever present threat posed to the English and English nation by the terrific violence of the continent. It is in the migratory and itinerant person of Juliet, however, that we can locate the Gothic heart of *The Wanderer*, as she haunts the southern shores of England, dislocated from her rightful inheritance and from her true identity (if such a thing might be said to exist in the world Burney portrays) – her marginal status in the world echoed in her drifting across littoral England.

Juliet's Channel crossing from the French coast to the English shore at the start of the text initiates her status as a Gothic migrant, as she is forced to adopt a bewildering range of cognomens to smuggle herself into English society, becoming in the process a strangely uncanny figure. Among her various names, she is known as: the Incognita, the Wanderer ('without even a name!'), an exile, L.S., Elless, Ellis, Julie, 'Citoyenne Julie', Juliet, 'a helpless foreigner', as 'no foreigner' (for 'I am English!') (Burney 1991: 33, 740, 214, 26). Designations such as 'Incognita' and 'Wanderer' certainly frame Juliet as a typically Gothic protagonist,[22] but what is perhaps most significant is the lack of stability her migration generates. Even her race becomes unsettled – or, more pertinently,

---

[22] On Juliet as a 'Gothic Wanderer' see Tichelaar (2012).

malleable – as she voyages from France to Britain: in the small boat that ferries her to England, her fellow passengers suggest she might well be 'a tawny Hottentot as a fair Circassian' (12), and her skin is seen to be 'of so dark a colour' that it 'might rather be styled black than brown' (19); yet on making landfall her skin is 'changed from a tint nearly black, to the brightest, whitest, and most dazzling fairness' (43). Her voice, too, is somewhat inscrutable: during her time in France, Juliet had 'perfectly retained her native tongue, though she had acquired something of a foreign accent' (643). Juliet is, Margaret Doody notes, 'both black and white, both Eastern and Western, both high and low, both English and French' (xv). Like a Gothic cipher, Juliet is intensely overdetermined. She is, one character notes, 'an adventurer and an impostor; with her blacks, and her whites, and her double face!' (251). To another, she is 'a swarthy minx', 'a mere imposter', and thus 'probably French' (830) – a clustering of notions that locate in a single body a range of Othernesses. To her English companions, she poses a Gothic problem, evoking what David Punter calls 'the cryptic impossibility of interpretation or translation which may be presented to us in certain circumstances by the body' (Punter 2016: 117). Juliet's transchannel existence renders her – and forces her to become – illegible and uncanny.

For Freud, the uncanny has to do partly with dislocation. Freud hypothesises that 'the uncanny would always be an area in which a person was unsure of his way around: the better oriented he was in the world around him, the less likely he would be to find the objects and occurrences in it uncanny' (Freud 2003: 125). Juliet's homecoming is disorienting and exilic. She returns to Britain in the belief that 'to touch the British shore would be liberty and felicity!' (Burney 1991: 751): the coastal arrival promises a transformation in fortune – yet this transformation is elusive because of Juliet's suspected Otherness and lack of clear connections to England. 'I feel myself', Juliet laments, 'though in my native country, like a helpless foreigner; unknown, unprotected' (214). When she becomes an émigrée, Juliet becomes her own uncanny double (doubled many times over, in fact), and her migration (back) across the Channel is all at once a form of emigration, a return (home), and an exile. Her existence on Britain's shoreline is meaningfully liminal or interstitial: though she makes landfall on the English coast, she is for the majority of the novel never quite *landed* – never quite at home or secure at the perilous and imperilled edge of the nation, and never quite in possession of her self. Juliet's e/immigration places her into a state of suspension, situating her in a littoral existence akin to that of the exiles of Charlotte Smith's *The Emigrants* (1793), who have become frozen, as it were, on Britain's coast, their gazes cast back towards France and their bodies perched precariously on England's cliff-edge.

Indeed, though the coast is an imagined site of 'liberty and felicity', Juliet in fact acknowledges that she ultimately failed to 'conceive ... the difficulties, dangers, disgraces, and distresses towards which I was plunging! (751). The constant sense of *sinking* and *plunging* that shapes Juliet's experience of England – of being 'plunged' into the 'depths of distress' (389) – associates Burney's wanderer less with the security and stability of land, and rather with the obscure oceanic depths across which she sails at the novel's opening – and into which she casts her wedding ring: these depths, like Juliet, are capable of concealing secrets. In this sense, Juliet's experience chimes with Caroline Emily Rae's recent theorisation of a littoral identity conceptualised via the idea of 'uncanny waters'. Literary figurations of uncanny waters – particularly those connected with the North Atlantic Littoral – 'offer a transoceanic dialogue that shifts constructions of subjectivity away from national and terrestrial boundaries to one more akin to the fluid and relational dialectics of transcorporeality' (Rae 2022: 64). For Rae, 'the uncanny arises in particular encounters with aqueous others (usually in the form of ghosts/doubles) who emerge on the shoreline to cast doubt on epistemologies and ontologies that frame the Northern Atlantic as a knowable and comprehensible space' (66). These Gothic subjects 'function as reminders of the material interconnection between humans and the ocean while simultaneously highlighting the legacy of colonialism and capitalism'; they provide a 'deterritorialising – de-*terra*-torialising – impulse that reorients bodies towards water' (66–67). Juliet, as a transchannel subject, has a body that points continuously elsewhere, conjuring up a wealth of associations, racial and national: her inscrutable person draws her English interlocutors into contemplation of the range of acknowledged or abjected Othernesses that might be said to constitute or underpin the English nation. The novel collapses high society and low society, whiteness and Blackness, and the English subject with the French citoyen(ne).

The Wanderer suggests that the 'uncanny waters' of the littoral world are an especially potent means of unsettling national identity or presumptions because of the region's continuous – and illicit – interchange with the world(s) beyond the nation. Indeed, the novel's smugglers, we learn, have 'agents all round the coast' (Burney 1991: 717), turning the entirety of the English coast into a potential site of dangerous insurgency – a potential realised when, for example, Juliet's French husband finally reaches the English coast, prompting a Gothic sequence of 'fainting, terrour, and excess of misery' (734). Moreover, littoral landings in *The Wanderer* involve not just the smuggling of goods or people but also *ideas* across the channel. Events in France do not merely cast Juliet upon English shores; a Revolutionary fervour also washes ashore, and those who succumb to it – most notably the character of Elinor – become estranged within the narrative and, like Juliet, littoral (and then global) wanderers. Elinor's fervent enthusiasm for the French Revolution – 'the finest thing in the world' (69) – alienates her from her love interest, Harleigh (whom Juliet ultimately marries), and in her increasingly deranged efforts to gain Harleigh's attentions, she casts herself in the role of a French émigré. She travels along the English coast, from Portsmouth to the Isle of Wight, procuring there 'a foreign servant' and 'some clothes of an indigent emigrant': 'She then dresse[s] herself grotesquely yet, as far as she could, decently, in man's attire' and adopts the persona of 'a foreigner, who was deaf and dumb' (395). Her disguise enables her to smuggle herself into a concert and upstage Juliet by publicly attempting suicide in front of Harleigh (an attempt that fails).

If the coast provides the means and communities by which Elinor can render herself an exile of the Revolution, the descent into madness that the narrative implies these actions signify finally entails a more profound and more permanent form of exile and eternal wandering than even Juliet has endured. Juliet and Elinor effectively trade places over the course of the novel: the suspected and uncanny foreigner is finally embraced as an English subject, and the English subject becomes an outcast Other. When Elinor finally sees the need to give up her pursuit of Harleigh, she departs from the coastal world and the narrative itself: 'Drive to the end of the world!' she tells her coachman as she takes her leave (797). Elinor initiates a willed Miltonic expulsion from Edenic England – because, as Kristen M. Distel has argued, she 'violates norms for Englishwomen's conduct and values' and 'fails to perform her national identity properly' (Distel 2020: 33, 36), because she has been affected by the Revolution. In this respect, too, the novel's reflections on the politics of migration redound finally on the English: what would it take, the novel wonders, for the Revolution to produce an English émigré(e)?

Despite early reassurances to Juliet that she has not merely been moved 'from one bad shore to another' (Burney 1991: 26), the English coast is shown throughout *The Wanderer* to be unnervingly proximate to the Revolution – the Channel, as one character puts it, is no more than a 'little canal' (257) – and littoral England is readily susceptible to transgressions by the Terror and its agents. Even efforts to embrace the coast in conventionally aesthetic terms are undercut by what Leya Landau has referred to as the 'Gallic identity' that marks Burney's English coastline (Landau 2018: 44). Halfway through the novel, Juliet follows a stranger to the coastal cliffs and teeters on the brink of sublime experience as she gazes across the sea: 'the expansive view, impressive, though calm, of the sea, and the awful solitude of the place, would have sufficed to occupy the mind of [Juliet], had it not been completely caught by the person whom she followed' (Burney 1991: 385). This person offers a French apostrophe to France, situated across the sea: 'Oh ma chère patrie! ... ne te reverrai-je jamais!' (385). The voice swiftly reveals the speaker to be Gabriella, Juliet's much-sought-after French companion and another émigrée who has recently buried her young son on this portion of the coast. Here, Landau notes, 'the English coast becomes newly defined through the imagined French shore and the narrative's fleeting view of the oceanic sublime' (Landau 2018: 44). What matters most in this encounter between two emigrants on England's coast is the way in which a typical sublime view of England's enchanting shores is rescripted by the political situation – and a sense that the English coast is not only a refuge for emigrants, but their sepulchre, a site of interment. The Burkean sublime cannot sustain itself in the face of the tragic forms of loss emanating from the Revolution beyond the sea. In *The Wanderer*, the English coastal world becomes uncanny as we are, to recall Freud, *dis*oriented. The text prompts us to orient ourselves afresh in a defamiliarised vision of littoral England – made even more so by the extended French dialogue that takes place between Juliet and Gabriella. The relationship between migration, foreign utterances, and the transformation of coastal communities is similarly significant to Conrad's tragic tale of emigration and wreckage, 'Amy Foster'.

4.2 Uncanny Utterance and Conrad's Littoral Other World

In Edward Said's influential judgement, Conrad's 'Amy Foster' offers 'perhaps the most uncompromising representation of exile ever written' in its portrait of 'a foreigner perpetually haunted and alone in an uncomprehending society' (Said 2003: 179–180). Conrad's tale follows the washing ashore on the Kent coast of a young Polish emigrant, the sole survivor of the wreck of a vessel carrying migrants from continental Europe to the United States. The emigrant – who is eventually known as 'Yanko Goorall' (the text defers and distorts his actual name in a manner akin to Burney's *Wanderer*) – struggles with acceptance and basic comprehension in the small rural coastal community in which he takes up residence. Though he eventually marries and has a son, his wife, Amy Foster, cannot endure Yanko's strange utterances; Amy finally abandons him, taking their child with her. Yanko shortly thereafter dies of a fever. Like Burney's Juliet, Yanko's emigrant status renders him strikingly illegible on the English coast: he is seen as 'a hairy sort of gipsy fellow', a 'nondescript and miry creature', 'a bit of a Hindoo', 'a Basque' – yet again a constellation of Gothicised Othernesses, heightened by the mysteriousness of his sudden appearance on the shore (Conrad 2022: 130, 131, 136). Where Burney's novel emphasises the illegibility and instability of the migrant *body*, Conrad's tale of migration and littoral community focuses on the uncanny valences of the migrant's *voice*. For Burney, Juliet's voice is a relatively consistent index of identity: when we first hear Juliet enter the novel, she speaks, and then 'the *same* voice' speaks again, and once more 'the *same* voice' calls out (Burney 1991: 11, emphasis added). Juliet's voice speaks to the *sameness* that inheres within her multiple guises, the kernel of her (ultimately unthreatening aristocratic English) identity. In Conrad, by contrast, the uncanny voice of the *foreigner* unsettles, while making profoundly visible, distinctions between self and Other, thereby eroding the possibility of maintaining communal and national identities through the exclusion of other selves and other identities.

For the purposes of this Element, it is worth noting that the date of publication (1901) situates Conrad's tale of emigration and coming-ashore into Britain alongside an abundance of *fin-de-siècle* Gothic invasion narratives (as highlighted in Section 3). Indeed, as the story of a migrant from 'the eastern range of the Carpathians' (Conrad 2022: 132), Conrad's story reads as a suggestive companion to Bram Stoker's *Dracula*. In a compelling reading of Stoker's novel, Attila Viragh has argued that Dracula might be read less as a colonist than 'a subaltern struggling against cultural loss', whose migration to Britain is shadowed by the Count's anxieties about fitting in: he is 'afraid that he will be unable to linguistically and culturally adapt to England, that he will stand out and be ridiculed for it' (Viragh 2013: 232–233). Yet Dracula undoubtedly remains a terrorising force in Britain, and where Stoker emphasises the Gothic horror of the shipwrecked immigrant from the Carpathians, Conrad locates the Gothic perspective more firmly within those English inhabitants of the coast who try to *read* and comprehend Yanko. That is, the English coastal world Gothicises the figure who is cast ashore: there is nothing inherently Gothic about the coastal arrival. Descriptions of Yanko as a 'miry creature' and 'gipsy fellow' might put us in mind of the Gothic figures found in *Frankenstein* and *Wuthering Heights* (1847). And we can see an anticipatory vision of the littoral spectre of 'Oh, Whistle, and I'll Come to You, My Lad' when we find Yanko stumbling awkwardly around the rural coastscape: the locals, we are told, 'saw him fall down, pick himself up, and run on again, staggering and waving his long arms above his head' (Conrad 2022: 131). Importantly, the text clearly states that this is what the *locals* 'saw': the eerie vision originates in the English populace, not in any objective perspective.

Read as a tale attuned to the Gothicisation of the coast, 'Amy Foster' quite clearly signals that, in the context of narratives of migration, the coast can be a zone of quite overwhelming horror, just as it is a zone of refuge; but the affective dimension of this horror is sadness, not terror. This is felt most powerfully when the bodies of Yanko's fellow travellers, 'his grisly company'

(126), are washed ashore. Following the wreck, the drowned migrants are lost – their tragedy concealed – in the ocean's depths:

> Then, after the tide turned, the wreck must have shifted a little and released some of the bodies, because a child – a little fairhaired child in a red frock – came ashore abreast of the Martello tower. By the afternoon you could see along three miles of beach dark figures with bare legs dashing in and out of the tumbling foam, and rough-looking men, women with hard faces, children, most fair-haired, were being carried, stiff and dripping, on stretchers, on wattles, on ladders, in a long procession … to be laid out in a row under the north wall of the Brenzett Church. (133)

Conrad's vision of a beach heaped with migrants' dead bodies speaks to an enduring aspect of the dangers and terrors that mark migrant experiences globally. The desolate scene of the migrant's perilous ocean crossing and mass drowning is counterpointed by the presence of the Martello tower: the image of a coast anxiously anticipating invasion undercut by the tragic coming-ashore of the dead.[23] As this event suggests, 'Amy Foster' emphatically figures the beach as, in the words of Virginia Richter, a site of 'disaster, death and the expulsion from the human community' (Richter 2020: 70). Conrad's tale resonates with the coastal Gothic's preoccupation with the beach as a site of annihilation. This is further compounded by Yanko's experience as a displaced migrant experiencing something like a living death on the Kent coast: Yanko's death at the tale's end finds, as it were, the earlier shipwreck and mass drowning catching up with him.

Against the mute spectacle of loss pictured on the beach, Yanko's voice stands out. The voice serves not, however, to tether him to the community who, as we see above, rush to the beach to attend the dead foreigners. Rather, the voice renders Yanko illegible, incomprehensible. The voice is 'so disturbing, so passionate, and so bizarre' (Conrad 2022: 144); we are told how he 'instilled a strangely penetrating power into the sounds of the most familiar English words, as if they had been the words of an unearthly language' (130); it is an 'insane, disturbing voice' (132). To his English neighbours, Yanko exhibits a powerfully Gothic utterance – a form of speech that commands attention, yet which unsettles, unsettling even the linguistic community in which he is attempting to participate.[24] At its most radical, we might hear in the voice of Yanko the voice from the margins that Homi K. Bhabha imbues with the power to 'evoke and erase [the nation's] totalizing boundaries' (Bhabha 1990: 300). Bhabha turns in particular to migrants and other minorities 'who will not be

---

[23] As Virginia Richter has highlighted, it is the implicit European *whiteness* of these migrant bodies that enables the narrator to 'mark[] their death, within a logic of racial hierarchy, as tragic' (Richter 2020: 66).

[24] I discuss the nature of 'Gothic utterances' at greater length in Packham (2021).

contained within the *Heim* of the national culture and its unisonant discourse, but are themselves the marks of a shifting boundary that alienates the frontiers of the modern nation'; they 'articulate the death-in-life of the idea of the "imagined community" of the nation' (315).

Thus, in the mouth of Conrad's migrant, the English language becomes 'unearthly', translated via uncanny defamiliarisation. In encounters with Yanko's foreign accent, the migrant's interlocutors seem to realise that, to recall Freud, 'we ourselves speak a foreign language' (Freud 2003: 125). Indeed, even Yanko's English companions are heard speaking 'an incomprehensible tongue' (Conrad 2022: 135): the suggestion here is that the voices are incomprehensible *to Yanko*, yet the remark is made by the implicitly colonialist English narrator, prompting us to consider the wider orbit of this process of defamiliarisation initiated in the littoral world by a foreign arrival. The text is marked by a panoramic incomprehensibility. While the English coastal community is certainly wary and hostile towards the figure of the migrant, what predominates across 'Amy Foster' is not so much a zealous nationalism – a vocal reassertion of the imagined integrity of the nation – but rather the more Gothic prospect of cultural as well as linguistic collapse. The failure in the end to make room for Yanko transforms the coastal world into an uncanny non-place, no longer entirely homely: the littoral world is an elsewhere, a place – in distinctly Conradian terms – detached from itself.

In Conrad's tale, England is, as Josephine McDonagh reminds us, 'not the place of departure, or even of return, but rather a detour en route to America': Yanko's wreckage 'makes England something like a desert island, where a traveller thrown off track, like Robinson Crusoe, might have ended up' (McDonagh 2021: 291). For Yanko, 'who knew nothing of the earth, England was an undiscovered country' (Conrad 2022: 126) – an allusion to Hamlet's thanatic realm. He seems 'like a man transplanted into another planet', 'separated by an immense space from his past and by an immense ignorance from his future' (140). In strikingly Gothic terms, Yanko's incomprehensible encounters with the English villagers are framed as encounters with the (un)dead. Their faces are 'the faces of people from the other world – dead people', and they are 'as closed, as mysterious, and as mute as the faces of the dead who are possessed of a knowledge beyond the comprehension of the living'; consequently, Yanko enters into 'an existence over-shadowed, oppressed . . . as if by the visions of a nightmare' (138). Conrad's tale articulates the multitudinous ways the coast – the notional point-of-entry into a nation – is really a gateway to some 'other world'. In 'Amy Foster', the nation is recessive, vanishing beyond the narrative's horizon, a thing upon which it is impossible for Yanko to finally make landfall. In other words, Conrad conjures a version of England as a place of living interment, an interstitial world populated by the living dead.

4.3 Oyeyemi: Sea, Salt, and Soucouyant

From its opening lines, Oyeyemi's *White is for Witching* similarly establishes coastal Kent as a site of (living) burial, participating thereby in a trope central to the coastal Gothic: 'Miranda Silver is in Dover, in the ground beneath her mother's house' (Oyeyemi 2010: 1). These remarks, spoken by Miranda's girlfriend, Ore Lind, offer one explanation for the mysterious disappearance of Miranda, which occurs at the end of Oyeyemi's novel. The house in question is the Silver family's racist sentient guesthouse, located near the white cliffs of Dover. This *unheimlich* home has, it seems, trapped Miranda somewhere within its walls – as it has previously held on to other Silver women, including Miranda's mother, grandmother, and great-grandmother – in order to separate the 'alabaster-white' (229) girl from Ore, a young Black girl, adopted by a white couple after her birth mother, a Nigerian migrant, began experiencing postpartum depression. Set at the turn of the twenty-first century and inspired by *Dracula* (Cousins 2012), Oyeyemi's Gothic novel looks to the coast – and an iconic symbol of Englishness, Dover's white cliffs – in order to interrogate and dismantle Britain's enduring imperialist, racist, and xenophobic national myths and (imagined) histories. At the centre of the novel are the efforts of the malicious guesthouse to expel from itself (and, implicitly, from the *unheimlich* nation) its non-white and foreign occupants. Haunting in this coastal world becomes a means of preserving an intolerant and stagnant (and delusional) form of white Englishness, an identity which is in reality, the novel suggests, an uncanny and vampiric living-death.

With its Dover setting and extended reflections on immigration and its bureaucracies, *White is for Witching* connects with earlier coastal Gothic texts like *The Wanderer* and 'Amy Foster' – all of which might be grouped together via what Sarah Ilott refers to, in the context of Oyeyemi's novel, as a 'Kentish' or 'Dover Gothic', 'a subgenre that critically engages with imperial Gothic's expression of fears of invasion through subversively redeploying its motifs', confronting 'the xenophobia and nationalism surrounding constructs of Britishness' (Ilott 2018: 227). The novel's temporal setting (c.2000) and date of publication (2009) also connect the text with socio-political climates marked by anti-migrant nationalism advocated by fascist and right-wing political parties.[25] In *Witching*, this role is played by the British National Party, who, though never seen directly, are leafletting throughout Kent, and whose flyers are used by the guesthouse to intimidate

---

[25] Oyeyemi's novel is also attuned to the experience of Kosovan refugees who came to Britain during the Kosovo War (1998–1999). Their exclusion from the imagined community of the nation operates, at least partly, through a linguistic distortion recalling 'Amy Foster': while thinking about a murdered Kosovan boy, Miranda admits 'She was not sure how to pronounce his name, not even in her head would the sound make any sense' (Oyeyemi 2010: 30).

Ore. The spectral nature of the group – the leaflets are the only sign that they have been present – signals the Gothicism inherent to English nationalism, an elusive entity that nonetheless manifests real terror. The centrality of Dover's white cliffs to the nationalist imaginaries was made clear when, in the year of *Witching*'s publication, Vera Lynn sought legal action against the BNP for using her music on a fund-raising compilation CD named for her 1941 wartime song, '(There'll Be Bluebirds Over) The White Cliffs of Dover' (Bates 2009). The cliffs were brought to the fore again, more notoriously, by the UK Independence Party during election campaigning in 2015: stood on a beach beneath the cliffs, the party's then-leader, Nigel Farage, unveiled a poster (Figure 4) featuring three escalators running up the white cliffs of Dover, in order to highlight Britain's immigration "crisis".[26] Largely indistinguishable from the messaging of the most reactionary of coastal Gothic fiction, the poster emphasises the fragility or precarity of what is supposed to be firm and fixed: a border, a boundary.[27]

In Oyeyemi's littoral world, the white cliffs function as part of a wider ingrained and repeatedly reenacted quasi-mythic conception of England. Miranda and her brother, Eliot, play games called 'Hitler Resistance Force' (Oyeyemi 2010: 19) and 'King Arthur's Court' (28); when Ore arrives at the University of Cambridge, she thinks 'it could be Camelot, or Lyonesse' (143) – the latter point-of-reference also bringing to mind the image of a nation submerged. And if the guesthouse functions as one form of fortress or bulwark

Figure 4 UKIP 2015 campaign poster.

---

[26] A video of the unveiling can be watched via On Demand News' YouTube channel: www.youtube.com/watch?v=sq0aG-S17FA.

[27] This poster essentially replicates a 2014 poster featuring a single escalator against the white cliffs, captioned 'No border. No control'.

against a perceived Otherness (when the Silvers arrive, it feels like 'we're in a castle' (18)), Dover also shows itself to be a town rife with similar structures. Dover Castle glowers across the sea, full of 'medieval court reconstructions' and 'First and Second World War army barracks' (224). The 'Immigration Removal Centre', too – the most transparent sign that the coast functions as a hostile and restrictive borderland for arriving migrants – is referred to as 'the Citadel' (115), a final line of defence against enemy forces. As Ilott has also noted, the guesthouse 'parallels the workings of the nefarious local detention centre and works as a national allegory for the reception of migrants and refugees in Britain' (Ilott 2018: 222). Indeed, the pervasive doublings rippling throughout Oyeyemi's account of littoral England conjure up a version of nationalism constituted by an eerie homogenising sameness: the centrality of *whiteness* to this sameness further serves to produce an uncanny Gothic blankness, rendering the white English subject largely unreadable, a haunting reiteration of past selves, bereft of individuating selfhood.

Eliot, for example, prides himself on dressing like everybody else, but wonders if the implication is that Dover is 'full of Eliot lookalikes, or that I was one of the lookalikes, a copy of some original anonymous guy' (Oyeyemi 2010: 60). Miranda, too, is perceived by herself and others as simply another double – of Eliot and her dead female relatives. When Ore encounters the ghosts of Miranda's family, she notices that 'They were alabaster-white, every one of them' (229), and Miranda finds it 'tiresome to see herself repeated so exactly' in these ghosts (236). Miranda's own whiteness is metaphorically shored-up via her pica, an eating disorder that compels her to consume chalk: through this consumption, Miranda internalises the whiteness (of the cliffs) that operates as a longstanding – yet fragile and crumbling[28] – symbol of English national identity. This very act, the novel tells us, is killing her. Somewhat like 'Amy Foster', Oyeyemi's *Witching* imagines the ways in which a closing-down of the littoral world to foreigners or difference is a self-destructive process. Moreover, there is no original to which these seaside doppelgängers might refer for reassurance. When Ore and the Silver siblings discuss the ancient origins of Britishness in 'Angles and the Saxons and the Druids and the Celts and the Picts and the ... Jutes' – an observation that knowingly stresses the centrality of foreign incursion to British history and identity – the Silver's Nigerian housekeeper, Sade, notes 'with a great deal of satisfaction' that 'They died out' (208). If the littoral edgeland of the nation is a fragile zone, crumbling into the sea, so too, on a temporal scale, have things eroded – a Gothic evacuation of the past and any 'original', leaving only the doppelgängers contemplating their own gradual erasure.

---

[28] On the cliffs' fragility see Ilott (2018: 213–220).

The most evocative coming-together of *Witching*'s various Gothic and nationalist symbols occurs during one of Miranda's nightmares. The dream begins with a ghostly encounter with Miranda's own vampiric double – a figure that we are later led to associate with the Caribbean soucouyant – looking exactly like Miranda except that its 'teeth were jagged' (78). Miranda flees into the streets which are 'strewn with bits of houses' (79) as if in the aftermath of a Second World War bombing raid. She runs towards the coast and sees the castle:

> Across the cliffs, Dover Castle was black. The sun was rising and the sea was changing colour, but the castle stayed within its lines, hunched in a black mess of shapes, and the vast bank of chalk it stood on seemed to stir in the water as if fighting the darkness that tried to climb down it.
> Miranda knelt . . . . Someone floated face down at the foot of the cliff. The sea refused to take the body far from the shore and contented itself with tossing the corpse back and forth between its gentler waves.
> *We died this morning*, she thought, then saw a scrap of colour. The body wore green. Whoever was floating, it was not her. (80)

The implicit terror of the nightmare is partly the contest it stages between blackness and whiteness, and its fantasy of the castle possessed by or transformed into 'a black mess of shapes'. But what to make of the body in the sea? This is yet another largely unreadable littoral figure. Miranda assumes it isn't her, because she always wears black, not green. But is it wearing green, or has it turned green? After Miranda's disappearance, Eliot does in fact worry that she will be 'found drowned, washed up at the foot of the cliff' (239). But if not a prophetic glance forwards, it may then be the drowned body of a migrant.

A connection between greenness, Blackness, and the oceanic is made explicit by the guesthouse after it first becomes aware of Ore. When Miranda says 'I'm in love', the guesthouse thinks 'Disgusting. These are the things that happen while you're not looking . . . . When clear water moves unseen a taint creeps into it – moss, or algae, salt, even. It becomes foul, undrinkable. It joins the sea' (194). The guesthouse, wilfully resisting the notion of Black Britishness, connects Blackness with the sea, and Blackness moreover with foreign bodies 'creep[ing]' into 'clear water' – moss, algae, 'salt, even'. From such overtly racist perspectives, the sea itself becomes an abject thing, a zone of horror, lapping at the nation's shores, upon which the nationalist must keep vigilant watch. In this respect, the novel registers England's transformed relationship with the oceans: as *Witching* shows more than once, the mythic narrative encoded in 'Rule, Britannia', with its seaborne imaginary, no longer holds water in contemporary England. In littoral England, the coastworld has abjected the sea: the town 'seem[s] to hold the [sea] back with its split brick and glass'

(114). In the language of the blue humanities and the ecoGothic, the text identifies a nationalist ideology that is infused with both a hydrophasia – a (desired) forgetting of oceanic space, history, and culture – and a hydro*phobia*. Yet, recalling the transformative power embodied in Caroline Emily Rae's notion of 'uncanny waters', the sea – particularly the *salt* sea – is also a means by which *Witching* mounts a challenge to the racism and xenophobia stemming from a resurgent English nationalism. This becomes apparent as the novel's interest in the soucouyant begins to dovetail with its reflections on immigration and the oceanic.

The vampiric soucouyant is introduced into the novel by Ore, through her reading of Caribbean folklore, and expanded on by Sade, whose Yoruba folk practices help mitigate the guesthouse's violence. On the novel's British coastal Gothic, the soucouyant maps a Caribbean Gothic and – via the creature's association with Yoruba culture – a wider Black Atlantic Gothic geography. But, if Miranda is or has become possessed by the soucouyant, the creature is not to be understood as a foreign invader in the vein of earlier vampire texts, but as a diagnostic tool, a piece of cultural exegesis that renders comprehensible the uncanny body of Miranda. To see Miranda as the soucouyant is thus also to reverse the politics of a Gothic novel like *Dracula*: the vampire is *already* in England – perhaps *is* England – and that which has been brought into the country can help exorcise it. Salt, we are told, is one means by which the soucouyant can be defeated: 'If I didn't believe in the salt', Ore says towards the end of the novel, 'I would be lost' . . . . Salt is true' (229). The traditional use of salt as a means of expunging evil from the home or community takes on particular significance within *Witching*'s coastscape: salt saturates the atmosphere in Dover, brought in on the sea. When the Silvers move to Dover, the children straightaway notice 'wet salt on the air' (16). When Ore visits Miranda in Dover, she observes that Miranda's bedroom is 'almost friendly, like being carried on salt water towards yourself' (213). Salt is restorative, buoyant, homely, even, and the relatively diffuse thematics of salt within the novel suggestively point towards the sea as a site of salvation or preservation. The coastal atmosphere is saturated by the very thing that the text identifies as able to extinguish the malign ideologies that have come to inhere at the fragile limits of the nation, made manifest as Gothic monstrosity.

Oyeyemi's novel never makes the point explicitly, but the trajectory of its narrative gently nudges its readers to adopt something akin to an oceanic perspective: to oppose the sense of the oceanic as polluted and pollutant, and acknowledge oceanic interrelations as both a fundamental part of the nation's global and imperial history and one way of thinking beyond the corrupted temporalities and ideologies that inhere within the inward- and backward-looking nation. The effort to contend with the English soucouyant becomes a means by which the littoral world of *White is for Witching* might be prevented from turning into the self-entombing littoral world of Lanchester's *The Wall*.

5 Conclusion: Lighthouses, Wreckage, and the Gothic

In June 2013, *Foghorn Requiem* was performed at Souter Lighthouse on England's north-east coast. This requiem – a collaboration between artists Lise Autogena and Joshua Portway and the composer Orlando Gough – made use of three brass bands, the horns of over fifty ships located just offshore, and the startling, disquieting sound of Souter's foghorn.[29] The purpose of the performance was to commemorate the vanishment of the foghorn from the archipelago's coastal soundscape – the last foghorns in Britain and Ireland having been decommissioned several years earlier. The culminating blast from the lighthouse's foghorn rippled through the coastal soundscape, a participant in its own death song: being drained of its final breath it 'sang in broken-throated keening, and when it no longer had the strength for that, it stuttered and wheezed' (Allan 2021: 3). The requiem is the sound of a defiantly haunted shore, a mournful site of loss and disappearance; the composition participates in what Isabella van Elferen has identified as the uncanny hauntologies that always inhere within music, especially its disjointed temporality – the 'pasts, presents and futures that music evokes and undoes' (van Elferen 2012: 177). By way of conclusion to this Element, I turn to coastal Gothic that treats the coast less as a realm of horror and terror, but rather as a locus of recuperation, somewhere, as in the music of the requiem, to begin weaving together the wreckage of past, present, and future in new ways; I do so via an examination of a key architectural feature of the coastal Gothic: the lighthouse.

5.1 Lighthouse Gothic

It is easy to appreciate the allure of lighthouses to the Gothic imagination: erected in zones of danger and wreckage, towering yet lonely strongholds, storm- and sea-swept, a resonance chamber full of eerie creaks and groans emanating from masonry and oceanic depths. In his history of British and Irish lighthouses, Tom Nancollas makes the unnerving observation that 'They stand between land and sea, strength and fragility, the defined and the undefined, the mythical and the real. They stand at the edges of our nation and the edges of our consciousness' (Nancollas 2019: 9–10). The lighthouse, this suggests, teeters

---

[29] The performance can be heard via the requiem's website: www.foghornrequiem.org/documentation.

between realms, the real and the unreal – and, more strangely, at the peripheral borderlands of nation and self.

The Gothic prospect of a lighthouse 'at the edges of our nation and the edges of our consciousness' finds expression in *The Lighthouse* (1855), a two-act drama written by Wilkie Collins, with additions by Charles Dickens. The play is set off the Cornish coast in the Eddystone Lighthouse – specifically the second iteration of this lighthouse built by John Rudyerd (Figure 5) – and at the heart of its action is the realisation, as one character succinctly puts it, that 'Something seems to have gone wrong among the three Light Keepers' (Collins 2013: 50). In its claustrophobic setting, the play indulges in familiar Gothic conventions, including the harbouring (and revelation) of family secrets and ghostly apparitions that eventually conform to the Radcliffean trope of the explained supernatural. But it is the prologue, written by Dickens, that best illuminates the lighthouse's Gothic standing; introducing us to Eddystone, it tells us:

Figure 5 Isaac Sailmaker, *Eddystone Lighthouse* (c.1708). © National Maritime Museum, Greenwich, London

Within it are three men: to these repair
In our frail bark of Fancy, swift as air!
They are but shadows – as the Rower grim
Took none but shadows in his boat with him
So be ye shades, and for a little space
The real world a dream without a trace. (31)

The imaginative voyage to the lighthouse – always, in British literature, a fraught process – is akin to a voyage to the underworld: the storyteller is Charon and the English Channel is the river Styx or Acheron. If, in the nineteenth-century British cultural imagination, Cornwall was something of a Gothic edgeland, the nation's peripheral Other, here we move even beyond those shores; the 'real world' of the nation drops away behind us, and we exist somewhere between 'the mythical and the real', becoming ourselves like 'shades'. The lighthouse enacts a process of spectralisation.

Yet, in the literature of terror, the lighthouse is far from a straightforwardly *Gothic* structure or a convenient vessel for ghostly conjurations and psychological breakdowns. Instead, I argue, the lighthouse has quite another function in coastal Gothic; as a counterpart to those enduring symbols of a terrorising medieval past, such as the castle or monastery, the lighthouse is a figure of modernity, a light amid the darkness. We can see the lighthouse operating in this way, for instance, in the writing of Walter Scott, Ann Radcliffe, and, more recently, and in slightly more complex ways, Alice Thompson. Thus, if one lineage of the lighthouse in Gothic media takes as its point of departure Edgar Allan Poe's unfinished tale 'The Light-House' (c.1849), and finds expression in work such as Collins' drama and, more recently, Robert Eggers' *The Lighthouse* (2019), I want to propose an alternative tradition that takes Radcliffe as its point of departure and becomes evident in such recent novels as Thompson's *Pharos* (2002), Emma Stonex's *The Lamplighters* (2021), and C. J. Cooke's *The Lighthouse Witches* (2021). This lineage adopts the lighthouse as a space conducive to meditations on loss and recovery, a restorative space, where grief and injustice may be, if not ameliorated, illuminated and brought into the open, recovered from the crypt.

5.2 A Defence against Wreckage

In 1814, Walter Scott undertook a voyage around the coast of Scotland and the northern coast of Ireland aboard the *Pharos*, travelling from Leith to Greenock as a guest with the Commissioners of the Northern Lights, who were making inspections of existing lighthouses and identifying possible locations for new ones: leading the team was Robert Stevenson, the famous lighthouse engineer and grandfather to Robert Louis Stevenson. Scott's journal of the cruise does much to elaborate a distinctly Gothic vision of the Scottish and Irish coastline. Scott writes often of the ruined castles and other fortifications that dot the coast, and observes the fragility of the coastline itself, recording that at Belhelvie 'a whole parish was swallowed up by the shifting sands' (Scott 1998: 10). In rather Crusoevian terms, he describes a coastal cave on the Isle of Egg that 'is strewed with the bones of men, women, and children' – and from which he pilfers a skull (88–89). Even the landscape is legible as Gothic architecture: caves and caverns 'assume the appearance of old Gothic ruins' (12). One especially deep cavern inspires Scott to opine that 'Imagination can figure few deaths more horrible than to be sucked under these rocks into some unfathomable abyss, where your corpse could never be found' (68). But if Scotland and Ireland have Gothic shores, the lighthouse stands out amid this ruinous wonder. Bell Rock Lighthouse is 'well worthy attention', for it is 'not only handsome, but elegant' and 'exquisitely fitted up' (9).[30] At Sanday, part of Orkney, Scott sees Start Point Lighthouse, which 'has been erected lately upon the best construction' and is 'far better than the house of the master of the Fair Isle, and rivalling my own baronial mansion of Abbotsford' (40). The lighthouse is part of the de-Gothicisation of the coast, the refashioning of the Gothic coast, not simply because the lighthouse is a modern structure but because it provides defence against future wreckage and desolation.

The role of the lighthouse in Gothic fiction as refuge from tyranny and Gothic edifices is especially pronounced at the conclusion of Ann Radcliffe's *A Sicilian Romance*. As in much of Radcliffe's writing, the primary topography of the novel is coastal; moreover, we learn from the opening sentence of the book to read the coast, like Scott does, as a site of ruinous Gothic splendour: 'On the northern shore of Sicily are still to be seen the magnificent remains of a castle' (Radcliffe 1993: 1). The lighthouse, which appears in the final chapter of the novel, is the castle's antithesis. At the novel's end, the tyrannical patriarch and wicked stepmother have been despatched, their plot has unravelled, and the abjected mother, supposed dead, has been miraculously brought back alive by one of her daughters from the tomb-like littoral caverns beneath the Castle Mazzini. As the valiant Ferdinand tries to ascertain the whereabouts of his family, he finds, in the midst of the darkness through which he rides, 'a red light waving in the wind: it varied with the blast, but never totally disappeared' (196). Following this flame, he discovers 'a lighthouse situated upon a point of rock which overhung the sea', within which are 'several persons, who seemed like himself to have sought shelter from the tempest' (196): here, Ferdinand

---

[30] It is politic for Scott to be polite about Bell Rock: the man responsible for its recent construction was his voyage companion, Stevenson.

rediscovers friends and family, including his long-lost mother. From the lighthouse, the group travels to the Italian mainland and abandons the Gothic castle, leaving it, as Alison Milbank writes, 'an emblem, in its seaside setting, of the biblical house built on sand' (Milbank 2014: 98). As a refuge from tyranny, Radcliffe's lighthouse offers more than an allegorical light amid the darkness. It is a site of radical reunion, where the dead might be restored to the living. Moreover, the lighthouse provides an architectural setting in which the family – the *idea* of family – might be refigured. *A Sicilian Romance* offers, in its conclusion, a vision of society in miniature, gathered not around the overbearing despotism of the patriarch (whose realm is the castle, a Gothic ruin-in-the-making), but the redeemed matriarch: from within the lighthouse, a new family history might be articulated, a defence against further wreckage.

Refiguring and re-articulating the nation's dreadful history, dredging such histories from the crypt and into the light, is a principal concern of Alice Thompson's 2002 Gothic novel, *Pharos: A Ghost Story*, named for the vessel on which Walter Scott sailed in 1814 (Germanà 2010: 149). Set in 1826 on the fictional Jacob's Rock, an island off Scotland's western coast, *Pharos* seeks, through the form of a ghost story, to articulate Scotland's historical involvement in the slave trade. The novel is haunted by the hope that hidden memories – of the self as much as the nation – can be drawn or forced into the light. We learn that a slave ship was once wrecked off the coast of Jacob's Rock and that a young girl on the island named Grace (mistaken throughout for a ghost) is the daughter of the wreck's only survivor, an African priestess who died in childbirth, and one of the lighthouse-keepers, Cameron, who raped Grace's mother. Moving primarily between the two architectural structures on the island – the lighthouse and a crypt encrusted with driftwood, shells, and seaweed – much of the novel's action is channelled through Lucia, a woman washed ashore and suffering memory loss. Lucia is, it transpires, probably the slave ship's figurehead, the 'evil spirit' of the ship, 'enacting revenge', brought to life through the combined powers of a lighthouse-keeper named Simon, Grace, and Grace's dead mother, for whom Grace serves as a living medium (Thompson 2002: 137). For Monica Germanà, the lighthouse functions ambivalently in *Pharos*, as a literal and symbolic source of light *and* site of concealed and barbaric histories, while Lucia is the disruptive presence who uncovers 'the bogus foundations of its moral structure' (Germanà 2010: 152). Thus, the lighthouse and Gothic crypt are not necessarily counterpointed forms, but fundamentally entwined and entangled, telling a singular history.

In its hidden chambers, the lighthouse functions as a gateway into the historical past, as geography and temporality come unstuck in its depths. In a fever-dream, Lucia follows the sound of drums into the lighthouse's oil cellar, where previously she has discovered evidence of Cameron's violence. Cameron's 'secret room' has vanished and has been 'replaced by a much larger room …. A throng of dark bodies filled it', in the middle of which is 'an eighteen-year-old woman. A priestess' (Thompson 2002: 132): Lucia has been projected into the midst of a Voodou ceremony somewhere in the Caribbean. The priestess commands '*Spirit take revenge*' (133) and Lucia is whirled back to Jacob's Rock. Cameron is swiftly 'arrested for aiding and abetting illegal slave trading' (149); but Lucia (or her ghost, if she is not one already) remains, haunting the lighthouse. The new keepers, we are told, 'grew used to seeing the ghost of a woman' (149). Yet:

> The ghostly spirit still did not know who she was or where she had come from. But she roamed the lighthouse now waiting for someone to claim her, to tell her who she was and why she was there. (150)

The lighthouse is a portal towards revelation, enabling the illumination of that which has been unjustly hidden from sight or wilfully forgotten. Further, the lighthouse accommodates the revenant presence, a fragment of the wreckage produced by the colonial power, and this remains visible to all who subsequently reside here; the text travels to the edges of the nation in order to speak to that which is a core part of the nation's identity.

But the novel sounds a troubling final note. Lucia is no surer of herself now than she was when she first awoke on the island's shore, and the keepers have become accustomed to her ghost, with the *meaning* of her haunting at risk of folding back into a generic tale of haunted shores. There is a sense, here, that we simply expect the coast to be a Gothic world of revenants and unquiet spirits. The coast's disquieting narratives, *Pharos* argues, must be met with an impulse not merely of accommodation but deliberate re-articulation, in order better to apprehend how these ghosts haunt not a liminal realm at the peripheries of the nation, somehow detached from history, but an environment central to the nation's history and identity. Attentive to the crypt and digging beneath the surface of the coast's superficial regimes, *Pharos* implicitly follows Jean-Didier Urbain's compelling imperative that, to see littoral space for what it is, 'We have to be astonished by the beach. Be surprised by its existence. Stop thinking of it as self-evident and start questioning its reason for being' (Urbain 2003: 27). Another way to put this is to find ways, like Crusoe, to become *Thunder-struck*, and to intuit the value of attending to the Gothic coast – that is, to the substantial literary tradition I have, here, termed the coastal Gothic, and also to the Gothic rhetoric through which coasts are so often imagined in political, social, and ecological discourse.

As *Robinson Crusoe*, *Pharos*, and the other texts discussed across this Element demonstrate, littoral zones exert a powerfully ambivalent force in cultural imaginaries. Littoral encounters with strangers, spectres, and unstable coastal terrain produce forms of Gothic experience predicated on disorientation and dislocation – temporally, spatially, and epistemologically. In the Gothic imagination, the coast is a space for letting one's guard down while simultaneously undertaking the frantic work of reinforcing the nation's defences; it is a space for coming undone, and beachgoers are apt to find themselves beside themselves at the seaside. Foregrounding the coast as an environment crucial to the articulation of national identities also helps us complicate understandings of the coast as a truly liminal realm. Attention to the Gothic rhetoric pervading accounts of this region illuminates how such liminality is foremost a condition imposed – often for political as well as aesthetic reasons – on the environment and, moreover, on those who find themselves suspended or exiled in it.

To end, it is perhaps helpful to return to two different ways of perceiving coasts, as articulated by two extremely influential dwellers at the water's edge. For Rachel Carson, the coast is felt above all as an eerie more-than-human domain, peculiarly unsympathetic towards human interlopers. Travelling across a beach at night, Carson perceives 'the darkness of an older world, before Man', the only sound 'the all-enveloping, primeval sounds of wind blowing over water and sand, and of waves crashing on the beach' (Carson 2021: 5). By contrast, and writing from a different disciplinary perspective, John R. Gillis writes that '*Homo sapiens* are best described as an edge species that has consistently thrived in the coastal ecotone', and that changes to human society have been 'consistently generated on edges rather than from interiors' (Gillis 2012: 4). Coastal Gothic finds the point at which such views begin to intersect, weaving together an ecoGothic perception of the ecotone's environmental qualities with a recognition of the centrality of the coast to political and cultural histories. It posits that humans – and enduring narratives of nationhood and identity – are indeed deeply imbricated in littoral environments, but uneasily so. Generative of epistemic upheavals, coastal Gothic unsettles narratives of insularity and national exceptionalism, as its haunting footprints and uncanny presences prompt the continuous reappraisal of the worlds, tangible and spectral, that constellate along the tideline.

References

Aickman, Robert, *Dark Entries* (Faber & Faber, 2014).
Alder, Emily, *Weird Fiction and Science at the Fin de Siècle* (Palgrave Macmillan, 2020).
Allan, Jennifer Lucy, *The Foghorn's Lament: The Disappearing Music of the Coast* (White Rabbit, 2021).
Allen, Nicholas, *Ireland, Literature, and the Coast: Seatangled* (Oxford University Press, 2021).
Anon., 'Narrative of a Fatal Event', *Blackwood's Edinburgh Magazine* 2.12 (1818), 630–635.
Aravamudan, Srinivas, *Tropicopolitans: Colonialism and Agency, 1688–1804* (Duke University Press, 1999).
Armitt, Lucie, 'Ghost-al Erosion: Beaches and the Supernatural in Two Stories by M. R. James', in Lisa Fletcher (ed.), *Popular Fiction and Spatiality: Reading Genre Settings* (Palgrave Macmillan, 2016), 95–108.
  and Scott Brewster, *Gothic Travel through Haunted Landscapes: Climates of Fear* (Anthem, 2022).
Arnold, Matthew, *On the Study of Celtic Literature* (Smith, Elder, 1867).
Ash, Eric H., *The Draining of the Fens: Projectors, Popular Politics, and State Building in Early Modern England* (Johns Hopkins University Press, 2017).
Auden, W. H., *Look, Stranger!* (Faber & Faber, 2001).
Baldick, Chris, Introduction to *The Oxford Book of Gothic Tales* (Oxford University Press, 1992), xi–xxiii.
Bates, Stephen, 'We'll meet again . . . in court. Dame Vera, 91, takes on BNP', *Guardian*, 19 February 2009. www.theguardian.com/politics/2009/feb/19/vera-lynn-bnp-cd-court.
Berberich, Christine, 'Europe in Britain: The Marginalised Voices of EU Migrants in Contemporary British Brexlit', in Berberich (ed.), *Brexit and the Migrant Voice: EU Citizens in Post-Brexit Literature and Culture* (Routledge, 2023), 31–45.
Bhabha, Homi K., 'DissemiNation: Time, Narrative, and the Margins of the Modern Nation', in Bhabha (ed.), *Nation and Narration* (Routledge, 1990), 291–322.
Brannigan, John, *Archipelagic Modernism: Literature in the Irish and British Isles, 1890–1970* (Edinburgh University Press, 2015).

Brown, Ian, 'Myth, Political Caricature and Monstering the Tartan', in Brown (ed.), *From Tartan to Tartanry: Scottish Culture, History and Myth* (Edinburgh University Press, 2010), 93–114.

Bulfin, Ailise, *Gothic Invasions: Imperialism, War and Fin-De-Siècle Popular Fiction* (University of Wales Press, 2018).

Burke, Edmund, *Reflections on the Revolution in France*, ed. L. G. Mitchell (Oxford University Press, 1993).

Burney, Frances, *The Wanderer; or, Female Difficulties*, ed. Margaret Anne Doody, Robert L. Mack, and Peter Sabor (Oxford University Press, 1991).

Carpenter, Kirsty, *Refugees of the French Revolution: Émigrés in London, 1789–1802* (Macmillan, 1999).

Carson, Rachel, *The Edge of the Sea* (Canongate, 2021).

Caserta, Silvia, *Narratives of Mediterranean Spaces: Literature and Art across Land and Sea* (Palgrave Macmillan, 2022).

Castricano, Jodey, *Cryptomimesis: The Gothic and Jacques Derrida's Ghost Writing* (McGill-Queen's University Press, 2001).

Colley, Linda, *Britons: Forging the Nation, 1707–1837*, revised ed. (Pimlico, 2003).

Acts of Union and Disunion (Profile Books, 2014).

Collins, Wilkie, *The Lighthouse: A Drama in Two Acts*, ed. Andrew Gasson and Caroline Radcliffe (Francis Boutle, 2013).

Connolly, Claire, 'Too Rough for Verse? Sea Crossing in Irish Culture', in Joep Leerssen (ed.), *Parnell and His Times* (Cambridge University Press, 2020), 243–267.

Conrad, Joseph, *The End of the Tether and Other Stories*, ed. Philip Davis (Oxford University Press, 2022).

Corbin, Alain, *The Lure of the Sea: The Discovery of the Seaside in the Western World, 1750–1840*, trans. Jocelyn Phelps (University of California Press, 1994).

Cousins, Helen, 'Helen Oyeyemi and the Yoruba Gothic: *White is for Witching*', *The Journal of Commonwealth Literature*, 47.1 (2012), 47–58.

Covington, Sarah, '"The odious demon from across the sea": Oliver Cromwell, Memory, and the Dislocations of Ireland', in Erika Kuijpers, Judith Pollmann, Johannes Müller, and Jasper van der Steen (eds.), *Memory before Modernity: Practices of Memory in Early Modern Europe* (Brill, 2013), 149–164.

'David Cameron: "Swarm" of migrants crossing Mediterranean', *BBC News* (30 July 2015), www.bbc.co.uk/news/av/uk-politics-33714282.

Dawson, Janis, 'Charlotte Riddell (1832–1906)', *The Green Book*, 20 (Samhain, 2022), 26–41.

Defoe, Daniel, *The Life and Strange Surprising Adventures of Robinson Crusoe* ... (Cassell and Co., 1896).

Robinson Crusoe, ed. Michael Shinagel, 2nd ed. (W. W. Norton, 1994)

Distel, Kristin M., '"Never, Most Certainly Never, Can I Perform in Public": Juliet and the Shame of Visibility in Burney's *The Wanderer*', *The Burney Journal*, 17 (2020), 21–41.

Duckert, Lowell, *For All Waters: Finding Ourselves in Early Modern Wetscapes* (University of Minnesota Press, 2017).

Eliot, T. S., *Collected Poems, 1909–1962* (Faber & Faber, 1974).

Estok, Simon C., 'Theorizing in a Space of Ambivalent Openness: Ecocriticism and Ecophobia', *ISLE*, 16.2 (2009), 203–225.

Fox, William, *Thoughts on the Impending Invasion of England* (M. Gurney, 1794).

Freed-Thall, Hannah, *Modernism at the Beach: Queer Ecologies and the Coastal Commons* (Columbia University Press, 2023).

Freud, Sigmund, *The Uncanny*, trans. David McLintock (Penguin, 2003).

Gaskell, Elizabeth, *Gothic Tales*, ed. Laura Kranzler (Penguin, 2000).

Germanà, Monica, *Scottish Women's Gothic and Fantastic Writing: Fiction since 1978* (Edinburgh University Press, 2010).

Giblett, Rod, *Landscapes of Culture and Nature* (Palgrave Macmillan, 2009).

Gillis, John R., *Islands of the Mind: How the Human Imagination Created the Atlantic World* (Palgrave Macmillan, 2004).

The Human Shore: Seacoasts in History (University of Chicago Press, 2012).

Harris, Alexandra, 'Seaside Ceremonies: Coastal Rites in Twentieth-Century Art', in Lara Feigel and Harris (eds.), *Modernism on Sea: Art and Culture at the British Seaside* (Peter Lang, 2009), 227–243.

Hau'ofa, Epeli, *We Are the Ocean: Selected Works* (University of Hawai'i Press, 2008).

Hill, Susan, *The Woman in Black* (Vintage, 2016).

Hughes, William, 'Introduction: The Uncanny Space of Regionality: Gothic Beyond the Metropolis', in Hughes and Ruth Heholt (eds.), *Gothic Britain: Dark Places in the Provinces and Margins of the British Isles* (University of Wales Press, 2018), 1–24.

Ilott, Sarah, 'Gothic Immigration: Kentish Gothic and the Borders of Britishness', in William Hughes and Ruth Heholt (eds.), *Gothic Britain: Dark Places in the Provinces and Margins of the British Isles* (University of Wales Press, 2018), 211–232.

James, M. R., *Collected Ghost Stories*, ed. Darryl Jones (Oxford University Press, 2011).

Jotischky, Andrew, *Crusading and the Crusader States* (Routledge, 2013).

'Judicial Review and Courts Bill: Second Reading', *Hansard*, 702, 226–227 (26 October 2021), https://hansard.parliament.uk/Commons/2021-10-26/debates/273F4D6A-291D-4A73-8D7B-D6BE51F8448E/JudicialReviewAndCourtsBill.

Kareem, Sarah Tindal, *Eighteenth-Century Fiction and the Reinvention of Wonder* (Oxford University Press, 2014).

Killeen, Jarlath, *Gothic Literature, 1825–1914* (University of Wales Press, 2009).

The Emergence of Irish Gothic Fiction: History, Origins, Theories (Edinburgh University Press, 2014).

Kipling, Rudyard, *A Song of the English* (Doubleday, Page & Co., 1909).

Kristeva, Julia, *Powers of Horror: An Essay on Abjection* trans. Leon S. Roudiez (Columbia University Press, 1982).

Lanchester, John, *The Wall* (Faber & Faber, 2019).

Landau, Leya, '"Unconscious of her own double appearance": Fanny Burney's Brighton', in Matthew Ingleby and Matthew P. M. Kerr (eds.), *Coastal Cultures of the Long Nineteenth Century* (Edinburgh University Press, 2018), 29–50.

Luckhurst, Roger, 'Brexit Gothic', in Rebecca Duncan (ed.), *The Edinburgh Companion to Globalgothic* (Edinburgh University Press, 2023), 322–336.

Machen, Arthur, *The White People and Other Weird Stories*, ed. S. T. Joshi (Penguin, 2011).

Marine Management Organisation, 'How to arrange a burial at sea in the UK marine area', *gov.uk*, updated 19 February 2024, www.gov.uk/guidance/how-to-get-a-licence-for-a-burial-at-sea-in-england.

Maturin, Charles, *Melmoth the Wanderer* (Penguin, 2012).

McDonagh, Josephine, *Literature in a Time of Migration: British Fiction and the Movement of People, 1815–1876* (Oxford University Press, 2021).

McEvoy, Emma, *Gothic Tourism* (Palgrave Macmillan, 2016).

Mentz, Steve, 'Brown', in Jeffrey Jerome Cohen (ed.), *Prismatic Ecology: Ecotheory beyond Green* (University of Minnesota Press, 2013), 193–212.

Milbank, Alison, 'Ways of Seeing in Ann Radcliffe's Early Fiction: *The Castles of Athlin and Dunbayne* (1789) and *A Sicilian Romance* (1790)', in Dale Townshend and Angela Wright (eds.), *Ann Radcliffe, Romanticism and the Gothic* (Cambridge University Press, 2014), 85–99.

Murphy, Patrick J., *Medieval Studies and the Ghost Stories of M. R. James* (Pennsylvania State University Press, 2017).

Nancollas, Tom, *Seashaken Houses: A Lighthouse History from Eddystone to Fastnet* (Penguin, 2019).

Owenson, Sydney, and Lady Morgan, *The Wild Irish Girl: A National Tale*, ed. Claire Connolly and Stephen Copley (Routledge, 2016).

Oyeyemi, Helen, *White is for Witching* (Picador, 2010).

Packham, Jimmy, *Gothic Utterance: Voice, Speech and Death in the American Gothic* (University of Wales Press, 2021).

'The Gothic Beach', in Ursula Kluwick and Virginia Richter (eds.), *Handbook of Littoral Studies* (De Gruyter, forthcoming 2026).

Passey, Joan, 'Ann Radcliffe's Influences and Legacies', in Clive Bloom (ed.), *The Palgrave Handbook of Gothic Origins* (Palgrave Macmillan, 2021), 121–134.

Cornish Gothic, 1830–1913 (University of Wales Press, 2023).

Peck, Imogen, 'Edgehill, Naseby, and the Ghosts of the Civil Wars', *Midland History*, 49.3 (2024), 269–284.

Phillips, Jonathan, *The Crusades, 1095–1204*, 2nd ed. (Routledge, 2014).

Potter, Madeline, 'EcoGothic Doubles: Ocean and Hell in Charles Maturin's *Melmoth the Wanderer*', *Gothic Nature*, 3: Haunted Shores (2022), 217–242.

Punter, David, *The Gothic Condition: Terror, History and the Psyche* (University of Wales Press, 2016).

Radcliffe, Ann, *A Sicilian Romance*, ed. Alison Milbank (Oxford University Press, 1993).

The Castles of Athlin and Dunbayne, ed. Alison Milbank (Oxford University Press, 1995).

Rae, Caroline Emily, 'Uncanny Waters', *Feminist Review*, 130 (2022), 61–77.

Reboul, Juliette, *French Emigration to Great Britain in Response to the French Revolution* (Palgrave Macmillan, 2017).

Richter, Virginia, 'Stranded. The Beach as Ultimate Destination in Joseph Conrad's *Amy Foster* and Thomas Mann's *Death in Venice*', in Carina Breidenbach et al. (eds.), *Narrating and Constructing the Beach: An Interdisciplinary Approach* (De Gruyter, 2020), 57–81.

and Ursula Kluwick, 'Introduction: 'Twixt Land and Sea: Approaches to Littoral Studies', in Kluwick and Richter (eds.), *The Beach in Anglophone Literatures and Cultures: Reading Littoral Space* (Routledge, 2016), 1–20.

Riddell, J. H. [Charlotte], *Idle Tales* (Ward and Downey, 1888).

Ross, Adrian, *The Hole of the Pit and By One, By Two and By Three* (Oleander Press, 2010).

Roy, Ian, 'England Turned Germany? The Aftermath of the Civil War in Its European Context,' *Transactions of the Royal Historical Society*, 28 (1978), 127–144.

Said, Edward, *Reflections on Exile and Other Essays* (Harvard University Press, 2003).

Samsung Singapore, 'See you seaweed! With Photo Assist', YouTube (5 June 2024), www.youtube.com/watch?v=bcQYvMmEVTM.

Scott, Walter, *The Voyage of the Pharos: Walter Scott's Cruise Around Scotland in 1814* (Scottish Library Association, 1998).

Shakespeare, William, *Henry IV, Part One*, ed. David Bevington (Oxford University Press, 1987).

Shelley, Mary, *Frankenstein*, ed. D. L. Macdonald and Kathleen Scherf, 2nd ed. (Broadview, 1999).

Shepherd, Mike, *When Brave Men Shudder: The Scottish Origins of Dracula* (Wild Wolf, 2018).

Smith, Andrew, *Gothic Fiction and the Writing of Trauma, 1914–1934: The Ghosts of World War One* (Edinburgh University Press, 2022).

Smith, Charlotte, *Major Poetic Works*, ed. Claire Knowles and Ingrid Horrocks (Broadview, 2017).

Spooner, Catherine, '"Dark, and cold, and rugged is the North": Regionalism, Folklore and Elizabeth Gaskell's "Northern" Gothic', in William Hughes and Ruth Heholt (eds.), *Gothic Britain: Dark Places in the Provinces and Margins of the British Isles* (University of Wales Press, 2018), 27–43.

Starmer, Keir, 'PM remarks at Immigration White Paper press conference', Gov.uk (12 May 2025), www.gov.uk/government/speeches/pm-remarks-at-immigration-white-paper-press-conference-12-may-2025.

Stoker, Bram, *Dracula's Guest and Other Weird Stories*, ed. Kate Hebblethwaite (Penguin, 2006).

Sunak, Rishi, 'PM Rishi Sunak's statement on the plan to stop the boats', Gov.uk (22 April 2024), www.gov.uk/government/speeches/prime-minister-rishi-sunaks-statement-on-the-plan-to-stop-the-boats-22-april-2024.

Talfourd, Thomas Noon, 'Memoir of the Life and Writings of Mrs. Radcliffe', in Ann Radcliffe, *Gaston de Blondeville* ... vol. 1 (Henry Colburn, 1826), 3–132.

Thompson, Alice, *Pharos: A Ghost Story* (Virago, 2002).

Tombs, Robert, *This Sovereign Isle: Britain In and Out of Europe* (Allen Lane, 2021).

Tichelaar, Tyler R., *The Gothic Wanderer: From Transgression to Redemption* (Modern History Press, 2012).

Uglow, Jenny, *Elizabeth Gaskell: A Habit of Stories* (Faber & Faber, 1993).

Urbain, Jean-Didier, *At the Beach*, trans. Catherine Porter (University of Minnesota Press, 2003).

Van Elferen, Isabella, *Gothic Music: The Sounds of the Uncanny* (University of Wales Press, 2012).

Viragh, Attila, 'Can the Vampire Speak?: *Dracula* as Discourse on Cultural Extinction', *English Literature in Transition, 1880–1920*, 56.2 (2013), 231–245.

Walpole, Hugh, *All Souls' Night* (Valancourt Books, 2016).

Walton, John K., *The English Seaside Resort: A Social History, 1750–1914* (Leicester University Press, 1983).

The British Seaside: Holidays and Resorts in the Twentieth Century (Manchester University Press, 2000).

Wedlich Susanne, *Slime: A Natural History*, trans. Ayça Türkoğlu (Melville House, 2022).

Wright, Angela, *Britain, France and the Gothic, 1764–1820: The Import of Terror* (Cambridge University Press, 2013).

Cambridge Elements

The Gothic

Dale Townshend
Manchester Metropolitan University
Dale Townshend is Professor of Gothic Literature in the Manchester Centre for Gothic Studies, Manchester Metropolitan University.

Angela Wright
University of Sheffield
Angela Wright is Professor of Romantic Literature in the School of English at the University of Sheffield and co-director of its Centre for the History of the Gothic.

Advisory Board
Enrique Ajuria Ibarra, *Universidad de las Américas, Puebla, Mexico*
Xavier Aldana Reyes, *Manchester Metropolitan University, UK*
Katarzyna Ancuta, *Chulalongkorn University, Thailand*
Carol Margaret Davison, *University of Windsor, Ontario, Canada*
Rebecca Duncan, *Linnaeus University, Sweden*
Jerrold E. Hogle, *Emeritus, University of Arizona*
Mark Jancovich, *University of East Anglia, UK*
Dawn Keetley, *Lehigh University, USA*
Roger Luckhurst, *Birkbeck College, University of London, UK*
Emma McEvoy, *University of Westminster, UK*
Eric Parisot, *Flinders University, Australia*
Andrew Smith, *University of Sheffield, UK*

About the Series
Seeking to publish short, research-led yet accessible studies of the foundational 'elements' within Gothic Studies as well as showcasing new and emergent lines of scholarly enquiry, this innovative series brings to a range of specialist and non-specialist readers some of the most exciting developments in recent Gothic scholarship.

Cambridge Elements

The Gothic

Elements in the Series

Gothic Voices: The Vococentric Soundworld of Gothic Writing
Matt Foley

Mary Robinson and the Gothic
Jerrold E. Hogle

Folk Gothic
Dawn Keetley

The Last Man and Gothic Sympathy
Michael Cameron

Democracy and the American Gothic
Michael J. Blouin

Dickens and the Gothic
Andrew Smith

Contemporary Body Horror
Xavier Aldana Reyes

The Music of the Gothic 1789–1820
Emma McEvoy

The Eternal Wanderer: Christian Negotiations in the Gothic Mode
Mary Going

African American Gothic in the Era of Black Lives Matter
Maisha Wester

Biography and the Trade-Gothic Author: The Case of Isabella Kelly
Yael Shapira

Coastal Gothic, 1719–2020
Jimmy Packham

A full series listing is available at: www.cambridge.org/GOTH

Printed by Integrated Books International,
United States of America